eat.shop san francisco 2nd edition

an encapsulated view of the most interesting, inspired and authentic
locally owned eating and shopping establishments in
san francisco and the east bay

researched, photographed and written by kaie wellman
cabazon books : 2010

table of contents

eat

shop

kaie's notes on san francisco

Let me begin by getting a little confusion out of the way. The first edition of *eat.shop san francisco* came out in the fall of 2005 and that book featured businesses in just San Francisco. Then in the fall of 2007 came the second edition, which was renamed *eat.shop sf bay area* to indicate that businesses from both SF and the East Bay were being featured, and it was "plus-size" featuring 130 businesses, instead of the normal 85. With this renaming came the confusion. Oi! Sooooooo, the decision was made to return to the original, clear as a bell title, *eat.shop san francisco,* featuring businesses in both SF and the East Bay. And though this book is really the third edition, it has to be noted as the second edition to match up with the title. Phew!

While working on this edition, there were a number of great places that were either in the process of opening, or not open or availble to shoot for one reason or another. They are all *eat.shop* worthy. Here's the short list. In SF: Saison, Site Glass, Schmidt's, Nombe, Baker and Banker, Terroir and Smuggler's Cove. In the East Bay: Commis and Elmwood Cafe.

Also good to note is the ever-growing food cart scene. You can follow @streetfoodsf to get some ideas or sfcartproject.com for schedules. And here's a couple of my recommendations: Creme Brulee Cart (@cremebruleecart), Soul Cocina (@soulcocina), Smitten Ice Cream (@smittenicecream), Gobba Gobba Hey (@gobbagobbahey), Toasty Melts (@toastymelts), Roli Roti (@roliroti) and Who's Your Daddy Bacon Potato Chips (@baconpotatochip).

Finally, If you find yourself in need of a some downtime from eating and shopping, here are some suggestions outside of that realm:

1 > *The Audium*: A place defined as an exploration of space in music, where aural sculptures are created. A one-of-a-kind SF experience.

2 > *Yerba Buena Center for the Arts*: Contemporary art has a hold on SF, and Yerba Buena is a great place to experience cutting-edge exhibitions and performances. It's also conveniently across the street from SFMoma, which is always a must visit.

3 > *Walking over the Golden Gate Bridge*: No joke, it's a breath-taking experience.

3 > *Taking a Drive*: Okay, this is out of San Francisco, but it's a gorgeous drive. Take 101 north and exit on Highway 1 as it heads west through Muir Woods up to Point Reyes.

about eat.shop

• All of the businesses featured in this book are locally owned. In deciding which businesses to feature, that's our number one criteria. Then we look for businesses that strike us as utterly authentic and uniquely conceived, whether they be new or old, chic or funky. And if you were wondering, businesses don't pay to be featured—that's not our style.

• A note about our maps. They are stylized, meaning they don't show every street. If you'd like a more detailed map, pick up a Streetwise map for San Francisco or we have an online map with the indicators of the businesses noted > map.eatshopguides.com/sf2. And a little note about exploring a city. The businesses we feature are mainly in neighborhoods within the urban core. Each of these 'hoods (and others that we don't cover) have dozens of great stores and restaurants other than the ones listed in this book.

• Make sure to double check the hours of the business before you go as they often change seasonally.

• The pictures and descriptions for each business are meant to give you the feel for a place. Don't be upset with the business if what you see or read is no longer available.

• Small local businesses have always had to work that much harder to keep their heads above water. During these rough economic times, some will close. Does this mean the book is no longer valid? Absolutely not! The more you use this book and visit these businesses, the better chance they have to stay open.

• The *eat.shop* clan consists of a small crew of creative types who travel extensively and have dedicated themselves to great eating and interesting shopping around the world. Each of these people writes, photographs and researches his or her own books, and though they sometimes do not live in the city of the book they author, they draw from a vast network of local sources to deepen the well of information used to create the guides.

• Please support the indie bookstores in San Francisco. To find these bookstores, use this great source: www.indiebound.org/indie-store-finder.

• *eat.shop* supports the *3/50 project* (www.the350project.net) and in honor of it have begun our own challenge (please see the back inside cover of this book).

• There are three ranges of prices noted for restaurants, $ = cheap, $$ = medium, $$$ = expensive

previous edition businesses

If you own the prevous editions of this book, make sure to keep them. Think of each edition as part of an overall "volume" of books, as the businesses not featured in this new edition are still am-a-zing! If a previous edition business does not appear on this list, it is either featured again in this edition, has closed or no longer meets our criteria or standards.

eat

1550 hyde
24th street cheese co
a16
aziza
bakesale betty
bar crudo
bar tartine
bi-rite creamery
biondivino
blue bottle coffee
bob's donuts
bocadillos
bombay ice creamery
boulette's larder
bourbon and branch
canteen
césar
cheese plus
chocolate covered
coi
crixa cakes
dosa
emmy's spaghetti shack
essencia
farmer brown
gialina
guerilla cafe
hotel biron
ici
la taqueria
liguria bakery
lovejoy's tea room
lucca delicatessen
mission pie
nopa
on the bridge
piccino

pizzaiolo
pizzeria delfina
pizzetta 211
range
ritual coffee
roadside bbq
rosamunde sausage grill
saigon sandwiches
sam's grill
seasalt
shanghai dumpling king
sociale
sophia cafe
spork
st. francis fountain
stella pasticceria
swan oyster depot
tadich grill
tamarindo
tartine bakery
thanh thanh cafe
the alembic
the blue plate
the candy store
the front porch
tokyo fish
true sake
underdog
vik's chaat corner
walzwek
weirdfish
yank sing
zante pizza
zuni cafe

shop

826 valencia
addison endpapers
al's attire
alla prima
arch
area
aria
article pract
atys
cactus jungle
cookin'
creativity explored
cris
dandelion
dema
delilah crown
(now gigi + rose)
dish
doe
double punch
egg & the urban mercantile
erica tanov
tantastico
fiddlesticks
flora grubb gardens
gamescape
goorin hat shop
harputs market
herringbone
hida tool
house of hengst
in fiore
kamei retaurant supply
lavish
march

mollusk surf shop
monument
my trick pony
nancy boy
nida
park life
paxton gate
peace industry
propeller
self edge
slash
stem
supple
tail of the yak
tal-y-tara tea & polo shoppe
the ark
the ribbonerie
the seventh heart
the wok shop
thomas e. cara
velvet da vinci
william stout books
x21
yone of sf
zoe bikini

where to lay your weary head

There are many great places to stay in San Francisco, but here are a few of my picks:

joie de vivre hotels
jdvhotels.com
standard doubles from $100
notes: there are 18 affordable, well-conceived and executed jdv boutique properties in sf and the east bay.
favorites: hotel tomo (funky, bright, japanese), good hotel (urban simplicity with a green edge) and
hotel vitale (modern luxe with glorious views of the bay)

crescent hotel
417 stockton street (union square)
888.817.9050 / crescentsf.com
standard double from $140
notes: where modern and classic meet

hotel palomar
12 fourth street (financial district)
415.348.1111 / hotelpalomar-sf.com
standard double from $170 restaurant: the fifth floor
notes: urban luxury in the center of the action

hotel frank
386 geary street (union square)
415.986.2000 / hotelfranksf.com
standard double from $240 restaurant: max's on the square
notes: retro glam

the huntington hotel & nob hill spa
1705 california street (nob hill)
415.474.5400 / huntingtonhotel.com
standard double from $185 restaurant: the big 4
notes: old world style on "top" of the city

some other options: hotel nikko (hotelnikkosf.com), the clift (clifthotel.com), the orchard hotel (theorchardhotel.com), hyatt regency san francisco (sanfranciscoregency.hyatt.com), w san francisco (starwoodhotels.com/whotels)

notes

adesso

house-cured meats and a hoppin' aperitivo scene
4395 piedmont avenue. corner of pleasant valley
510.601.0305
mon - wed 5p - midnight thu - fri 5p - 1a sat noon - 1a

opened in 2009. owner / chef: jon smulewitz
$-$$: all major credit cards accepted
aperitivo. dinner. full bar. late night. first come, first served

piedmont > e01

I know there's a big world of happy hours out there, but I can't bring myself to partake in them because I have a lurking fear of chafing dishes and half-warmed potato skins sprinkled with bac-o-bits. Then there's the *aperitivo* at *Adesso*. This I can embrace, as does a good chunk of Oakland it seems, judging by the packed house. The *aperitivo* is an Italian style happy hour, where you buy the drinks and *Adesso* provides heaping platters of finger foods including their in-house cured salumi. Italians think the *aperitivo* stimulates the appetite for your dinner... sounds good to me.

imbibe / devour:
blood orange smash
07 etna rosso, firriato, sicilia
endless list of house-cured salumi
duck liver in scatola pate
arancini of pork ragu
sardines en saor
prosciutto & mozzarella di bufalo piadina
fried rock cod, tarragon & lemon panini

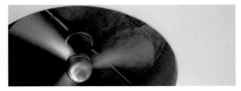

anthony's cookies

addictive cookies

1417 valencia street. between 25th and 26th
415.655.4834 www.anthonyscookies.com tw: @anthonyscookies.com
mon - sat 10a - 8p sun 10a - 6p

opened in 2009. owner: anthony lucas
$: all major credit cards accepted
treats. first come, first served

mission > **e02**

As I walked into *Anthony's Cookies*, I saw a guy sitting at a table with a glass of milk and a pile of cookies. It was somewhat unusual to see such a big dude eating this quintessential little kid's snack. After I ordered an assortment (I never eat just one cookie—it's detrimental to my health), I sat down near the cookie dude. We got to chatting and he told me he worked nearby and that he visited *Anthony's* three times daily. He had fallen madly, irrevocably in love with these warm, chewy rounds. He had clearly entered the cookie zone. And I merrily joined him.

imbibe / devour:
strauss milk
cookies:
  semi sweet chocolate chip
  cookies & cream
  cinnamon sugar
  toffee chip
  german chocolate
  banana walnut

bar bambino

essential wine bar and café
2931 16th street. between mission and van ness
415.701.8466 (VINO) www.barbambino.com tw: @barbambino
see website for hours

opened in 2007. owner: christopher losa chef: elizabeth binder
$$: all major credit cards accepted
lunch. dinner. brunch. reservations accepted

mission > e03

I find myself getting suspicious when somebody gushes about something. Are they being paid to be so positive? Is their discerning radar a bit skewed? Yet, here I am ready to gush about *Bar Bambino*. I really love this place. Love love love. And last I checked my offshore bank account, Christopher is not paying me to say so. What's got me in such a lather? This is the type of spot that's fantastic because it comes without pretense, and yet is carefully considered from the thoughtful wine list to a cheese selection gorgeously displayed in it's own glass room to the simple Italian cuisine. Love.

imbibe / devour:
selection of over 175 wines
house & artisanal cured meats
artisanal cheeses
olive oil flight
egg, truffle salt & parmigiano-reggiano bruschette
cestini stuffed with oxtail
puglian style braised lamb shank
napoleon of huckleberry semifreddo

bar jules

charming little neighborhood bistro

609 hayes street. corner of laguna
415.621.5482 www.barjules.com
lunch wed - sat 11:30a - 2:30p dinner tue - sat 6 - 10p brunch sun 11a - 2:30p

opened in 2007. owner / chef: jessica boncutter
$$: all major credit cards accepted
lunch. dinner. brunch. first come, first served

hayes valley > e04

When I arrived at *Bar Jules* to take pictures, the doors had yet to open for the night. So I plopped myself down at a outside chair. Then a man showed up. He looked at the door. He looked at me. And then he stood right in front of the door, intent on being the first person to enter *Bar Jules*. I understood his determination. Jessica has created a perfect little bistro where the food is spot on and the atmosphere cozy, with the perfect amount of buzz. By the time I left, the man was tucking into his main course, a look of contentment on his face.

imbibe / devour:
la bête pinot noir
fresh mint tisane
chickpea soup with cumin
house-cured sardines with new potato salad
wood-grilled california white sea bass with
    cauliflower, capers & chilis
muscovy duck breast with figs & polenta
wood-grilled skirt steak

benkyodo

japanese confectionary
1747 buchanan street. at scott
415.922.1244 www.bekyodocompany.com
mon - sun 8a - 5p

opened in 1906. owners: ricky and bobby okamura
$: cash only
treats. breakfast. lunch. first come, first served

japantown > **e05**

I'm constantly searching for places that feel like they are part of a bygone era. At *Benkyodo*, what caught my attention was the 1970s style fountain counter. I could imagine coming in here in '77 in my white San Francisco Riding Gear jeans to have a tuna melt and a Fresca. But the real story of *Benkyodo* is the mochi and manju that are made on site. Suyeichi Okamura began making these Japanese confections in 1906. Now over 100 years later, his grandsons are running the show. This is a great example of bygone not being gone at all, but better than ever.

imbibe / devour:
manju:
  dorayuki
  fukusa
  chofu
  kuri goma
  kinako
  pink habutae
fountain counter

boccalone

tasty salted pig parts
1 ferry building, #21. end of market street
415.433.6500 www.boccalone.com tw: @boccalone
mon - fri 10a - 6p sat 8a - 6p sun 11a - 5p

opened in 2009. owner / chef: chris cosentino owner: mark pastore
$-$$: all major credit cards accepted
lunch. dinner. online shopping. first come, first served

embarcadero > e06

I am a designer and with that comes a ridiculous obsession with packaging. The first time I visited *Boccalone*—the purveyor of artisanal salumi—I loved the packaging, but because it was so well done and sharp, I worried that the product might be secondary to the outer casing. Wrong, wrong, wrong on my part, and I was told so by most of the food community in SF. Chris is no poser (as those who have eaten at his other venture, *Incanto*, know). He's curing meats the right way: small batch production using darn good pigs, which as the tagline states, makes tasty, salted pig parts. Yes indeed.

imbibe / devour:
salumi cones
muffaletta sandwich
la cicciolina sandwich
salumi:
  lardo
  brown sugar & fennel
  nduja
easton's breakfast sausage

boot and shoe service

sibling rivalry creates great pizza

3308 grand avenue. between 580 and mandana boulevard
510.763.2668 www.bootandshoeservice.com
tue - thu 5:30 - 10p fri - sat 5 - 10:30p

opened in 2009. owners: charlie holliwell and richard weinstein chef: colin etezadi
$$: all major credit cards accepted
dinner. full bar. first come, first served

lower hills > e07

I know a whole bunch of adults who still have inferiority complexes in conjunction to their older sibling. What's up with that? I'd bet my last dollar that this isn't going to be an issue with *Boot and Shoe Service*, the latest offspring of Charlie Holliwell, whose first spot *Pizzaiolo* is worshipped in the East Bay. If anything, *BSS* is giving its sib a run for its money, as the place is packed from the moment the doors open. The pizza has a darn good char and the toppings are fresh and seasonal. Even if the name is a bit goofy (like calling your kid Moon Unit), this sibling has got it going on.

imbibe / devour:
the salty witch
smoking lillies
crudo of fluke with avocado & watermelon radish
fritto misto of asparagus, onion & fennel
pizza:
  margarita
  wild nettles & ricotta salata
canoli

brown sugar kitchen

new style, down-home cooking

2534 mandela parkway. at 26th
510.839.7685 (SOUL) www.brownsugarkitchen.com tw: @brownsugarkitch
tue - sat 7a - 3p sun 8a - 3p

opened in 2008. owner / chef: tanya holland
$-$$: all major credit cards accepted
breakfast. lunch. first come, first served

oakland > e08

On March 4th, 2010 my first waking thought was, "I'm going to *Brown Sugar Kitchen* this morning." My morning routine, which is usually blurry and slow at best, more resembled Usain Bolt heading for the shower. I was on the Bay Bridge in 20 minutes flat, and sitting at the counter here 10 minutes after that. Five minutes later I had my order in for cheese grits with poached eggs AND a waffle. 20 minutes later I was rubbing my full belly, feeling like the day had started on a supremely good note. *Brown Sugar Kitchen* done me good.

imbibe / devour:
brown sugar blend coffee
apple cider syrup
beignets & handmade jam
organic cheddar cheese grits & poached eggs
cornmeal waffle with brown sugar butter
fried oyster po-boy
brown sugar pineapple glazed baby back ribs
sweet potato pie

cam huong

fresh, fast banh mi and other vietnamese delights

920 webster street. between ninth and tenth
510.444.8800
mon - sun 7a - 7p

$: cash only
breakfast. lunch. dinner. first come, first served

oakland > **e09**

When I'm hungry, especially between the hours of noon and 3pm, I have a difficult time waiting for food to be made. This is when I am at the apex of my need for immediate "I need it right now" gratification. In other words, a slow food lunch makes me grumpy. In this situation, heading for *Cam Huong* makes a ton of sense. Here I can order a delicious curry chicken *banh mi* and have it in my hot little hands in less than a minute. Oh happiness, oh joy. And what really makes me trill in delight is that I'm only out three bucks or so. A food grinch no more.

imbibe / devour:
banh mi:
  curry chicken
  grilled beef onion roll
  shredded pork with fish sauce
  pork sausage
  vegetarian
shrimp muffin with pork & beans
shrimp, pork, daikon & carrot dumplings

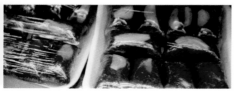

camino

a wood-oven wonderland
3917 grand avenue. at boulevard way
510.547.5035 www.caminorestaurant.com tw: @caminooakland
see website for hours

opened in 2008. owner / chef: russell moore owner: allison hopelain
$$: all major credit cards accepted
dinner. full bar. brunch. reservations recommended

Is it inappropriate to bring up fetishes in this book? Maybe so, but I think I'll do it anyway. I have a wee bit of a cookie fetish (see page 11) and also the clichéd female shoe fetish. My husband's dirty little secret is that he deeply desires a wood-burning oven in the kitchen. When I walked into *Camino*, I knew this place would make him burn with envy. Russell has not just one oven, but two, where he cooks about 99% of his menu. The smells of a veritable cornucopia of fresh vegetables and meats being cooked over an open flame are almost sinful.

imbibe / devour:
tequila blanco, cherry brandy, lime, grapefruit
pisco, lemon, egg whites, hibiscus bitters
local sardines with mashed garbanzo beans
grilled spring onion, roasted carrot & lentil salad
dungeness crab soup with saffron, lime & chile
asparagus with black trumpet mushrooms & egg
wood oven roasted pear stuffed with
   hazelnuts & almonds

canyon market

great neighborhood grocery
2815 diamond street. corner of chenery
415.586.9999 www.canyonmarket.com tw: @canyonmarket
daily 7a - 8p

opened in 2006. owners: richard and janet tarlov
$-$$: all major credit cards accepted
grocery. deli. first come, first served

glen park > **e11**

In my opinion, every neighborhood should have a great little market. Unfortunately this is not the reality of our world anymore, though in SF there are a number of fantastic grocers, including *Canyon Market* in Glen Park. This neighborhood, with its miniature main street and go-to spots like *Gialina* (featured in *eat.shop sf bay area*), the newly opened gift store *Perch*, *Modernpast* and *Bird & Beckett*—is a charmer. But the cherry on this hood's sundae is this perfect grocery. Not too big, not too small and featuring a mix of well-sourced products and their own line of goods.

imbibe / devour:
tule duck red ale
equator coffee
clover farmstead butter
bellwether farms sheep's milk yogurt
alhema d queiles olive oil
juanita's homemade buñuelitos
fresh baked bread & focaccia
great deli case

chilango

wholesome mexican food
235 church street. at market
415.552.5700 www.chilangococina.com
daily 11a - 10p

opened in 2009. owner: victor juarez chef: roberto aguiar-cruz
$-$$: all major credit cards accepted
lunch. dinner. first come, first served

castro > e12

If you live in or visit San Francisco, it is imperative to know a good place for a proper Mexican breakfast. Nothing starts a day right, or tempers a good old-fashioned hangover quite like huevos rancheros or migas or papas con huevos. Here's my suggestion: Go to *Chilango* and order any of the above mentioned dishes (I went for the papas). Get a side order of guacamole which looks like it took five goliath avocados to make, take a big forkful of the guac and plop it on your eggs, then douse the dish with Cholula. Total breakfast perfection.

imbibe / devour:
bohemia beer
guacamole chilango
cocktail de camaron
papas con huevo
duck flautas
huarache chilango
pambazo
chocolate mexicano

contigo

a food love letter to barcelona

1320 castro street. corner of 24th
415.285.0250 www.contigosf.com tw: @contigosf
tue - sat 5:30 - 10p sun 5:30 - 9:30p

opened in 2009. owner / chef: brett emerson owner: elan drucker
$$: all major credit cards accepted
dinner. reservations recommended

noe valley > **e13**

Some places, from the moment you walk in the door, have L-O-V-E written all over them. I don't mean in a romantic sort of way, I mean in an "the owners must really adore what they do" type of way. I felt this the moment I entered *Contigo*. Elan and Brett were warm and welcoming, and families with pipsqueaks happily co-mingled with Gen Y types. I positioned myself at the bar so I could watch the cooks in action making their Spanish/Catalan dishes. And when some of those dishes came my way, here's what was written on my face: L-O-V-E.

imbibe / devour:
isastegi sagardo naturala cider
penedès raventos i blanc cava
jamón ibérico de bellota pata negra
escarole salad with apples & fatted calf bacon
calamars a la panxa with cara cara oranges
oxtail croquetas
four course menu del dia
chocolate caliente con churros

dynamo donut + coffee

modern donut outpost
2760 24th street. between york and hampshire
415.920.1978 www.dynamodonut.com
tue - sat 7a - 5p sun 9a - 4p

opened in 2008. owner: sara spearin
$: cash only
treats. first come, first served

mission > **e14**

maple glazed bacon apple $

lemon thyme $2

sticky bun $3

vanilla bean $2

coconut $2.50

I think that Sara should have named her dee-lish-us donut spot Dy-no-mite so I could do my pathetic Jimmie Walker impression. Alas, she didn't ask me and named it *Dynamo Donuts + Coffee* which still gets the point across that these fried rounds of dough are outta this world. Even though I'm suspect of donut shops that make wacked out, stoneresque flavours like Nyquil glazed, I fully embrace Sara's creative recipes that taste amazing. The maple glazed bacon apple is hugely satisfying and should be considered a healthy meal, being that it covers four of the six food groups.

imbibe / devour:
four barrel coffee
ginger lemonade
donuts:
  maple glazed bacon apple
  lemon thyme
  coconut
  chocolate star anise
  candied orange blossom

ferry plaza farmers market

one of the top farmers markets in the country
1 ferry building. end of market
415.291.3276 www.ferrybuildingmarketplace.com/farmers_market.php
tue 10a - 2p thu 10a - 2p sat 8a - 2p

opened in 1992
$-$$: cash only
open air market. first come, first served

embarcadero > e15

TOKYO TURNIPS

CRANBERRY BE
#8/#

According to data that I dug up on on this thing called the internet, I learned that there were about 1700 farmers markets nationwide in 1994, and as of last year that number had tripled. That's impressive growth. In this region, there are plenty of farmers markets to choose from and because I can't list them all, I'm going to pull one out of the hat: the *Ferry Plaza Farmers Market*. Open three days a week, it's the perfect size to navigate. Here's where I go to get Happy Girl tomato juice, which is like sucking on a fresh tomato, and a 4505 golden dog zilla style. Soooo good.

imbibe / devour:
some favorite vendors:
happy girl kitchen
4505 meats
scream sorbet
st. benoit yogurt
della fattoria
county line harvest
dirty girl produce

flour + water

neopolitan style pizza and fresh pasta
2401 harrison street. corner of 20th
415.826.7000 www.flourandwater.com tw: @flourandwater
daily 5:30p - midnight

opened in 2009. owner / chef: tom mcnaughton
owners: david steele and david white
$$: all major credit cards accepted
dinner. reservations accepted

mission > **e16**

In this era of scrimping and saving, there's been an explosion of spots serving simple, affordable foods: burgers, sandwiches and the ever popular pizza. SF and the East Bay are crawling with pizza joints, some of them appearing in the previous editions of this book: *Pizzeria Delfina*, *Gialina*, *Piccino* and *Pizzaiolo,* to name a few. So when it came time for this edition, who would make the cut? In SF, *Flour + Water* is the pizza and pasta hot spot du jour. Whether you choose an inspired-by-the-motherland pie or a savory bowl of tajarin, or in my case, both, you can't go wrong.

imbibe / devour:
08 weingut niklas sudtiroler lagrein
yellowtail with radish & meyer lemon aioli
pizza:
   biancoverde
   salsiccia
   topinambur
artichoke & potato tortelli
fennel ice cream with prosecco gelee

four barrel coffee

purveyors of fine coffees

375 valencia street. between 14th and 15th
415.987.7119 www.fourbarrelcoffee.com tw: @fourbarrel
mon - sat 7a - 8p sun 8a - 8p

opened in 2008. owner: jeremy tooker
$: all major credit cards accepted
coffee. treats. first come, first served

mission > **e17**

I'm not going to lie to you and say that I am an expert on the caffeinated bean called coffee. I'm one of those woosy folks whose system started revolting against caffeine and now orders a decaf soy latte that's closer to flavored baby formula then a true cuppa joe. Sad, but true. I am, though, surrounded by experts when it comes to the bean and the drink that's extruded from it and many are besotted by *Four Barrel Coffee*. Jeremy is a disciple of St. Duane of *Stumptown,* and his coffee, roasted in the back of this loft-like space, echoes it.

imbibe / devour:
four barrel roasts:
   colombia el jordan reserva
   sumatra blue batak
   friendo blendo espresso
cup-at-a-time drip
single origin espresso
cappuccino
dynamo salted caramel donut

frances

modern california cuisine

3870 17th street. between noe and sanchez
415.621.3870 www.frances-sf.com
tue - thu, sun 5 - 10p fri - sat 5 - 10:30p

opened in 2009. owner / chef: melissa perello
$$-$$$: all major credit cards accepted
dinner. reservations recommended

noe valley > **e18**

As a child I remember that one of the lessons that was drilled into me was, "Don't play favorites." And though I've got this lesson embedded in my mind, I'm ignoring it in *Frances's* case. I'm not going to be coy about how much I adore this place. What's so great about it? Let's start at the top. Melissa makes delicious food that is pristine, but not pretentious. The staff is as good as they come; highly professional, but still über-friendly. The room is small and chic in an understated type of way, yet still cozy. Yes, I'm going to play favorites—I love *Frances*.

imbibe / devour:
07 marco felluga pinot grigio
half & half refresher
frances iced coffee
local dungeness crab salad
applewood smoked bacon beignets
bellwether farm ricotta gnocchi with green garlic
sonoma duck breast with butter bean ragout
lumberjack cake

humphry slocombe

artisan ice cream with a sense of humor
2790a harrison street. corner of 24th
415.550.6971 www.humphryslocombe.com tw: @humphreyslocombe
daily noon - 9p

opened in 2008. owner / chef: jake godby owner: sean vahey
$: cash only
treats. first come, first served

mission > **e19**

One of the problems with getting older is not being up on the slang of the day. I suspect that I might have been one of the last people to know the term "hot mess." Though I think this is a wickedly useful adjective (most mornings I am one), I feel ridiculous saying it, except when I go to *Humphrey Slocumbe* and order the sundae of the same name. This is one delicious edible wreck involving vanilla ice cream, butterscotch, bananas and yes, oh yes, marshmallow fluff. Don't stop here though, as there are many other inventive flavors to try and I suggest trying them all.

imbibe / *devour:*
bourbon & coke float
ice cream:
  tin roof sundae
  peanut butter curry
  autumn harvest corn
  mcevoy olive oil
  brown sugar yogurt
boccalone lard caramel

il cane rosso

casual rotisserie

1 ferry building, #41. end of market street
415.391.7599 www.canerossosf.com tw: @canerossosf
see website for hours

opened in 2009. owners: daniel patterson and lauren kiino chef: douglas borkowsk
$-$$: all major credit cards accepted
lunch. dinner. brunch. first come, first served

embarcadero > 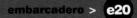 e20

I'm slightly embarassed to admit that of all of the tempting items (and there are many) on *Il Cane Rosso's* menu, the first thing that caught my attention was the Straus Dairy vanilla soft serve. Though I'm thinking a visit to a food shrink would be helpful to figure out this attraction, I came to my senses quickly and ordered the porchetta. Oh holy pig, it was good. *Il Cane Rosso* is the creation of Daniel of *Coi* fame and Lauren, and it's hard not to love their take on the small sandwich shops and rotisseries of Southern Italy. Just think of it as slow food served in a flash.

imbibe / devour:
fentiman dandelion-burdock soda
scrimshaw pilsner
spit-roasted porchetta
marin sun farms beef stracotto
warm soul food farm egg salad sandwich
roasted carrots & parsnips
olive oil fried friarelli & padron peppers
three-course family style dinners

jai yun

a unique chinese dining experience
680 clay street. between kearney and montgomery
415.981.7438 http://jaiyun.menuscan.com
lunch mon - wed, fri 11:30a - 2:30p dinner mon - wed, fri - sun 6:30 - 9:30p

opened in 2002. owner / chef: nei' chia ji
$$-$$$: cash only
lunch. dinner. reservations recommended

downtown > e21

Though dozens of restaurants in SF's Chinatown are happy as all get out to serve kung pao chicken to the tourist trade, it's not so easy to find a place to have a meal that truly excites the senses. Thank Buddha there is *Jai Yun*. Here's how it works. Call and make a reservation so Chef Nei' knows how many he's cooking for at that meal. Once seated a member of the wait staff, who doesn't speak much English, will ask if you want the $15, $25 or $35 meal. Then sit back and wait for the magic. Multiple small courses will appear, each more delicious than the last.

imbibe / devour:
multiple course meal that could include:
  chinatown special cabbage
  vegetarian goose
  lotus root salad
  poached chilled duck
  foo yung abalone
  green bean lasagna with chinese ham
  crispy eggplant with scallions

la palma mexicatessen

tortilleria y huaracheria
2884 24th street. corner of florida
415.647.1500 www.lapalmasf.com
mon - sat 8a - 6p sun 8a - 5p

opened in 1953. owner: castano family
$: visa. mc
breakfast. lunch. dinner. grocery. deli. first come, first served

mission > **e22**

Though people usually go on and on about Mission-style burritos when they are talking about Mexican food in this city, I can get a whopper of a gas attack just thinking about those five pound bricks. What really rocks my boat is a good tortilla. You can watch them being made at *La Palma Mexicatessen* (I love this name), along with many other delights, like handmade masa, perfect for taking home and turning into tamales. There's something about this food that makes you feel like you have your very own Mexican grandmother lovingly making it for you.

imbibe / devour:
handmade tortillas
nacatamales
papusas
tripas
masa
tacos de canasta
huarache
chicharron

lers ros

non·americanized thai

730 larkin street. between o'farrell and ellis
415.931.6917 www.lersros.com
daily 11a - midnight

opened in 2008. owner / chef: tom silargorn
$-$$: visa. mc
lunch. dinner. late night. delivery. first come, first served

tenderknob > e23

For the food obsessed, it's important to define and search out places that are authentic—in other words, places that have not been overly sullied by the American palate. One cuisine that foodies desire a pure experience with is Thai, and they are often disappointed in their quest. That was until *Lers Ros* opened. Here's a menu that has items like duck larb, house special frog and garlic and pepper rabbit. Can you imagine the joy of the SF fooderati when they discovered Tom's cooking? I'm amazed there wasn't a ticker tape parade down Van Ness.

imbibe / devour:
chrysanthemum drink
chang beer
look chin phing
yum koh moo yang
poh-tak
khao na phed
pad ped nok
yum pak karrd dong

little skillet

farm fresh soul food

360 ritch street. between brannan and townsend
415.777.2777 www.littleskilletsf.com tw: @littleskillet
mon - sat 9a - 3:30p

opened in 2009. owners: jay foster and deanna sison chef: christian ciscle
$: cash only
breakfast. lunch. first come, first served

soma > **e24**

When I'm working on these books, there are high points and low points. Though I could regale you with the lows (frat boy hot tubbers), I'd rather focus on the highs. Eating *Little Skillet's* fried chicken and waffles on a sunny spring morning, sitting on a loading dock in a SoMa alley was way high on the happy scale. Though this place is no more than a window attached to a kitchen the size of small dorm room, it puts out realllllly good Southern-style food. Which makes sense because the good folks of *Farmer Brown* are behind the venture.

imbibe / devour:
blue bottle coffee next door at *centro*
blackberry lemonade
egg mcmahon
chicken & waffles
grits with bacon, brown sugar & pecan
meatloaf po' boy
waffledog
mini pecan pies

local 123

good coffee for the east bay
2049 san pablo avenue. between university and addison
415.517.8694 www.local123cafe.com tw: @local123cafe
mon - fri 6:3a - 7p sat - sun 7a - 7p

opened in 2009. owners: katy safle and frieda hoffman
$: visa. mc
coffee / tea. light meals. first come, first served

berkeley > **e25**

Growing up in Portland, Oregon, I had a certain vision of Berkeley which included hippies, Alice Waters and people hanging out in coffee shops reading important pieces of literature. I've come to see over the years that this vision might be slightly askew, though Berkelites do like a mellow place to take a load off and sip a good cup of brew. New to the scene here is *Local 123*, and the locals are embracing it. Not only are they serving Healdsburg-based Flying Goat coffee, they are also making some tasty sustenance. All told, a very Berkeley sort of place.

imbibe / devour:
flying goat coffee
mumbai chai
bionade
rosemary cheddar scone
sandwiches:
  the eggman
  the walrus
  salty goat

miette pâtisserie & confiserie

my favorite place

449 octavia street. between linden and hayes
1 ferry building, #10. end of market
415.626.6221 / 415.837.0300 www.miette.com / www.miettecakes.com
see website for hours tw: @miettecakes

opened in 2001. owner: meg ray
$-$$: all major credit cards accepted
treats. first come, first served

hayes valley / embarcadero > **e26**

It was a bitter day when I learned late last year that *Miette Confiserie* off of Hayes was going to close. I bought a bag of goodies and took a long look at my dream candy store one last time. One tear escaped. Okay, that's not true. But what is true is when I revisited this area in March, I walked past *Miette* to mourn a bit, and jeepers!, it was open. Then I almost did cry. This is one of the prettiest spots to ever grace the pages of *eat.shop*, and Meg's baked goods are dee-vine. And did I tell you they are making cotton candy to order? Thank you sugar gods for answering my prayers.

imbibe / devour:
chocolate tomboy cake
mini scharffen berger cakes
rose geranium parisian macaron
banana cream tart
lemon verbena cotton candy
robin's eggs
au coeur des chocolates sea salt caramels
mast brothers chocolate

·moscow & tbilisi bakery

great russian bakery

5540 geary boulevard. between 19th and 20th

415.668.6959

mon - sat 7a - 9p sun 9a - 7p

$: cash only

bakery. deli. first come, first served

inner richmond > **e27**

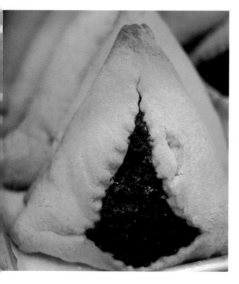

Here is the perfect, kooky San Francisco snapshot. I pulled my car into a rare Inner Richmond weekend parking spot so I could go to the great Russian bakery, *Moscow & Tbilisi*. As I exited the car, a "Jingle Bells" serenade began coming from an elderly, toothless Asian man playing the accordian. Ahhh, yes—nothing like a continuous loop of annoying holiday jingles in March to put a grin on your face. What made me even more chipper was what was inside. Big, fat piroshkis and piles of brightly colored meringues and baked goods galore. Merry Christmas to me!!

devour:
chocolate potato log
halal breads
piroshki
borscht
katchapuri
walnuts in grape juice
blinses
poppy seed hamentashen

namu

where californian cuisine meets up with the flavors of asia
439 balboa street. between fifth and sixth
415.386.8332   www.namusf.com   tw: @namusf
sun - tue 6 - 10:30p wed - sat 6p - midnight pulutan weekdays 9:30 - 10:30p

opened in 2007. owner / chef: dennis lee owners: daniel and david lee
$$: all major credit cards accepted
dinner. pulutan. reservations accepted

inner richmond > 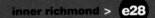 **e28**

Fusion is a word that strikes fear in the hearts of many eaters, myself included. Whoever thought that marrying the flavors of the Caribbean with those of Italy should be locked up in the bad food idea jail. On occasion *Namu* has been called a fusion restaurant, but I would beg to differ. My take is that it's a place where the flavors of Korea, Japan and Thailand beautifully collide with the clean and healthy notes of Californian cuisine. This is super invigorating food that I could eat everyday. And though I am a card-carrying carnivore, *Namu's* menu is filled with vegetable dishes that put meat to shame.

imbibe / devour:
thai chili soju infusion
sake flights
daily crudo with pickled battera konbu
shiitake dumplings in a dashi mushroom broth
lamb chops, thai basil pesto, sambal
seasonal korean style hot pot
namu ice cream sandwich
pulutan (free food with purchase of alcohol)

nopalito

sustainable organic mexican kitchen
306 broderick street. between oak and page
415.437.0303 www.nopalitosf.com tw: @nopalitosf
daily 11:30a - 10p

opened in 2009. owners: allyson and laurence jossel and jeff hanak
chefs: gonzalo guzman and jose ramos
$-$$: all major credit cards accepted
lunch. dinner. first come, first served

lower haight > e29

There are many corners of this city that are food destinations, but the intersection of Broderick and Oak covers a number of bases. First head for *Nopalito* which was inspired by the staff meals at *Nopa* that Gonzalo and Jose cooked. The owners of *Nopa* recognized the simple brilliance of the duo's Mexican dishes and *Nopalito* came to be—SF has gone mad for this place. After cleaning your plate (like I did), if you realize your fridge is empty, go next door to *Falletti Foods* / *Delessio Market & Bakery* to stock up. It's a one-stop dining and shopping experience.

imbibe / devour:
hibiscus valencia orange sparkling drink
chile chocolate milk
panucho de pollo al pibil
tamal en pipianodo de puerco
quesadilla azul con hojas de chicharo y hongos
ceviche verde de pescado y calamari
mole poblano con pollo
caldo tlalpeño

outerlands

warmth, shelter, food and friendship

4001 judah street. corner of 45th
415.661.6140 www.outerlandssf.com tw: @outerlandssf
tue - sat 11a - 3p, 6p - close sun 10a - 2:30p

opened in 2009. owner / chef: dave muller
$-$$: visa. mc
lunch. dinner. brunch. first come, first served

outer sunset > **e30**

It's a Sunday morning, and I've got a Saturday night tv hangover. Though the sun is out, everything seems muted in my fuzzy world as I make the drive towards Outer Sunset. Everything changes though when I sit down in the wooden-planked *Outerlands*. The smells from Dave's kitchen are ridiculous: brewing coffee mingling with the heavenly scents of fresh-baked bread and bacon frying. Suddenly the sun is bright and everything is in Technicolor. All I see are smiling people—even those waiting to get into this little beachside nirvana. Happiness is a meal at *Outerlands*.

imbibe / devour:
hot ginger lemon apple cider
chemex drip siteglass coffee
baked eggs with rosemary
eggs in jail
dutch pancake
goat cheese souffle
hot open faced crimini mushroom sandwich
pink lady apple crisp

sandbox bakery

asian inspired bakery

833 cortland avenue. corner of gates
415.642.8580 www.sandboxbakerysf.com tw: @sandboxbakery
mon - fri 6a - 3p sat - sun 7a - 3p

opened in 2009. owner / baker: mutsumi takehara
$: all major credit cards accepted
coffee / tea. treats. first come, first served

bernal heights > **e31**

I'm sitting here playing a word association game with myself. Cow = milk. Chocolate = more, please. Morning pastry = yuzu and sage. Say what? Okay, the only reason I made that leap was because of *Sandbox Bakery*. As I was standing in front of the case of baked delights here, some of them Asian inspired, I was drawn to the yuzu marmalade and sage pan. Okay, I was looking at about ten other things also, but this is what I went for, and I'm glad I did. Not too sweet, with the perfect hit of sagey herbalness—it rocked my early morning world.

imbibe / devour:
chai / espresso hybrid
valrhona mocha
yuzu marmalade with sage pan
melon pan
chocolate banana hearts
sweet cheese croissant
swiss dill biscuit
pig in a blanket

sebo

the fine art of sushi

517 hayes street. near octavia
415.864.2181 www.sebosf.com tw: @sebosf
tue - sat 6 - 10p sun izakaya 6 - 11p

opened in 2006. owner / chefs: michael black and danny dunham
$$-$$$: all major credit cards accepted
dinner. first come, first served

hayes valley > 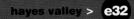 e32

This is another one of those eating experiences that I could get gushy about, but I'm thinking I'll show some restraint. I really really really like *Sebo*—a lot. With that nugget of understatement on the table, I'll move on and explain. *Sebo* is the type of place that needs no hype nor hojive. It's all about the freshest and most interesting varities of fish available. And when it gets into the capable hands of Michael and Danny, they honor it with a stellar and often simple preparation. If you are looking for beautiful sushi without the hyperbole, *Sebo* is up your eating alley.

imbibe / devour:
orion beer
jinyu brave warrior sake
chef's selection sashimi
sakamushi (sake & butter steamed clams)
nigiri:
  aoyagi (stimson clam)
  hirame (fluke)
  ainame (greenling)

singapore malaysian

the name of the restaurant says it all
836 clement street. between ninth and tenth
415.750.9518
mon, wed - thu 11:30a - 3p, 5 - 9:30 fri - sun 11:30a - 9:30p

opened in 1989. owner: the tan family
$: visa. mc
lunch. dinner. first come, first served

inner richmond > e33

The hawker stalls of Singapore are one of my favorite places to eat on earth. I could do a long laundry list of beloved foods at these stalls, but I'll just name a few for the sake of time and your attention span: popiah, char kway teow, hainanese chicken and rice and fish head curry. Problem is, it's hard as heck to find this type of food—that's just as good—in the States. Hence why I swooned over *Singapore Malaysian*. No name fluffing here—just a straightforward moniker that lets you know the cuisine you will be devouring. Now I won't have to buy that zillion dollar ticket back to Singapore.

imbibe / devour:
cendol
tiger beer
otak-otak
pou pia
ikan belendang
singaore chow bee hoon
hainan chicken & rice
bu bocha cha

73

spqr

the flavors of italy
1911 fillmore street. between pine and bush
415.771.7779 www.spqrsf.com tw: @spqrsf
see website for hours

opened in 2007. owner: shelly lindgren chef: matthew accarrino
$$-$$$: all major credit cards accepted
dinner. brunch. full bar. reservations recommended

pacific heights > 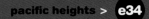 e34

When a restaurant first opens, there are a whole lotta obstacles. The hope is that good press will come and with that, a full house. But what happens when the honeymoon ends and/or some of the original team move on? This is what happened at *SPQR*. When it opened in '07, the buzz was deafening as this was the same team behind the beloved *A16*. But after the initial glow, Chef Nate Appleman left for the Big Apple. Shelly then showed her mettle by bringing in the talented Matt to helm the kitchen, and the second coming of *SPQR* blossomed. Some argue it tops *SPQR v.1*. Whatever. It's just plain good.

---

imbibe / *devour:*
08 elena walch, gewürztraminer, alto adige
fritto misto of local sole & fall vegetables
eggs al diavolo
baked ricotta, cucumber, radish & pine nuts
duck ravioli, dolcetto sour cherries & sage
stinging nettle torchio, garlic crema & pancetta
brown butter torta, meyer lemon curd &
  sicilian pistachios

summer kitchen bake shop

charming take-away spot
2944 college avenue. between ashby and russell
510.981.0538 www.summerkitchenbakeshop.com tw: @summerkitchen
daily 10:30a - 9p

opened in 2009. owner / chef: greer nuttal owner / baker: charlene reis
owner: paul arenstam
$-$$: all major credit cards accepted
breakfast. lunch. dinner. treats. first come, first served

berkeley > e35

I'm married to a guy who thinks the most relaxing thing in the world is to come home and cook a big dinner, happily and wantonly using every pan in the kitchen to create something delicious. I love him and I love his food, but sometimes I just want to get take-out. Meaning I want something simple, yet delicious, that doesn't require 42 pans to make (and wash). *Summer Kitchen Bake Shop* to the rescue. I can already smell the fried chicken. And though the other half might grumble, I know he would approve. And if he doesn't, no cupcake for him.

imbibe / *devour:*
house-made pure cane sugar soda
herbed egg omelet sandwich
new orleans muffaletta
fulton valley fried chicken
hobb's pepperoni pizza
mole poblano
gingerbread sliced loaf cake
vanilla cupcakes with vahlrona pearls

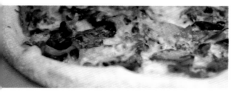

tcho

chocolate as a cure-all

pier 17. at green
415.963.5056 www.tcho.com tw: @tchochocolate
daily 10a - 6p

opened in 2008. owner: timothy childs
$: visa. mc
treats. first come, first served

embarcadero > **e36**

Some people eat an apple a day, some people pop vitamins each morning for vigor, but my health regimen requires a *Tcho*-a-day. Though this prescription might seem a wee bit out of the ordinary, I highly recommend it. What could be better for the body than a good dose of dark chocolate? If you read *Tcho's* website it uses big words like Theobromine and Phenethylamin to talk about the health benefits. If you want the quick translation, these words mean "quit reading and eat the chocolate, dummy." Which is what I did and I'm aglow. I'm a *Tcho* believer.

imbibe / devour:
tcho chocolate:
  hot chocolate
  organic baking drops
  tcho-a-day: 30 / 60 / 90 supply
  chocolate-drenched mango
  roasted nibs
  dark chocolate flavors:
  fruity, citrus, nutty & chocolatey

the sandwich joints of san fran

where to get your sandwich on

naked lunch: 504 broadway. kitchenette: 958 illinois street
pal's takeaway (inside tony's market): 2751 24th street
nl: 415.577.4951 / pt: 415.203.4911 see websites for hours
www.nakedlunchsf.com / www.kitchenettesf.com / www.palstakeaway.com

nl > owner / chef: ian begg owner: ryan maxey
k >owner / chefs: douglas monsalud and brian leitner
pt >owner / chef: jeff mason owner: david knopp
lunch. first come, first served

north beach / dogpatch / mission > **e37**

There are a number of sandwich joints that have been popping up all over the Bay Area in the last year like gophers at a golf course. I checked out just about every one of note, and ate a solid 20 pounds of sandwiches. But when it came time to choose, I couldn't. Each place had mastered the art of putting interesting, delicious ingredients between the outer wrapping of bread. So I whittled down my favorites to *Kitchenette*, *Naked Lunch* (pix were taken here) and *Pal's Takeaway*, three totally different spots in three corners of the city. Best of luck choosing your favorite.

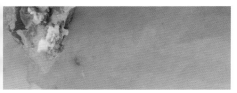

devour:
kitchenette:
  grilled korean-style bavette steak sandwich
  grilled mushroom banh mi
naked lunch:
  foie gras torchon & duck prosciutto sandwich
  piquillo pepper & manchego sandwich
pal's takeaway:
  moroccan lamb with feta & mint salsa sandwich
  southern lao minced chicken laab sandwich

true burger

an old-fashioned burger modernized
146 grand avenue. at valdez
510.208.5678 www.trueburgeroakland.com tw: @trueburger
see website for hours

opened in 2010. owner / chefs: greg eng and jason law
$: cash only
lunch. dinner. first come, first served

oakland > **e38**

Sometimes a good thing shouldn't be messed with. Case in point, the classic American cheeseburger. Though I'm not going to diss all the half-pounders with their fancy fromages and focaccia buns, my burger preference veers towards the type you get at a drive-thru. Yes foodies, I like American cheese on my burger. And this is why I heart *True Burger*. Greg and Jason have big restaurant cred, but they thought the Bay Area needed a classic burger made with good ingredients and love. Throw in some of drive-in favorites like milkshakes and fries, and happy days are here again.

imbibe / devour:
strawberry milk shake
sprecher cream soda
cheesy trueburger with griddle onions
'shroom burger
housemade chili-cheese dog
chopped blt salad
spiced dill pickle
hot fudge sundae

vintage berkeley

affordable artisanal wines

2949 college avenue. between ashby and russell
510.549.9501 www.vintageberkeley.com
see website for hours and other locations

opened in 2005. owners: peter eastlake and michael werther
$-$$: all major credit cards accepted
tastings. events. classes. first come, first served

berkeley > e39

I have a chequered history with wine. My first memories of the grape came in the form of the boxed wines of the '80s, consumed by my parents on ski trips. Then there was the Annie Green Springs varietal (lemon satin country cherry, anyone?) that popped up in college. Against all odds, I married into a family that sells wine for a living. Ten years later I'm still learning, but I can spot a great wine shop and *Vintage Berkeley* fits the bill. At their striking retail spaces, you can find an eclectic array of wines, most under $25, from around the world. You'll never consider Two Buck Chuck again.

imbibe:
cava avinyo brut reserva nv, penedes
09 cep (peay vineyards) rose, sonoma coast
08 gulfi rossojbleo nero d'avola, sicily
07 copain syrah "tous ensemble," mendocino
06 chateau coupe roses minervois
07 chateau du hureau saumur champigny
vina do burato ribeira sacra

wexler's

modern bbq

568 sacramento street. corner of montgomery
415.983.0102 www.wexlerssf.com
mon - fri lunch 11:30a - 2:30p tue - sat dinner 5 - 11p

opened in 2009. owner: matt wexler chef: charlie kleinman
$$: all major credit cards accepted
lunch. dinner. reservations recommended

financial district > e40

I know that I've already blah-blah'd about this, but I can get pretty wrapped up in the packaging of things, and if the outer wrapping seems a bit too slick, I become suspicious. So you would think my radar would be up in accordance to *Wexler's* where the food is Southern barbeque inspired, but the décor is urban cool with a massive ceiling installation that looks like a long, undulating black wave. But these details just add to the allure here, as does Charlie's food where he puts an uptown spin on some seriously down home food. Suspicions averted, I'm hooked.

imbibe / devour:
north coast brewing pranqster ale
basil haydens scotch
zuckerman farm shaved asparagus salad
county line little gems salad
bbq california quail
smoked short rib
bourbon banana cream pie
chocolate chili fudge pie

no. beach •

jackson •
square

chinatown •

financial •
district

embar-
cadero •

eat

e6 > boccalone
e15 > ferry plaza
farmer's market
e20 > il cane rosso
e21 > jai yun
e36 > tcho
e37 > the sandwich joints
of san fran
e40 > wexler's

shop

s9 > carrots
s12 > eden & eden

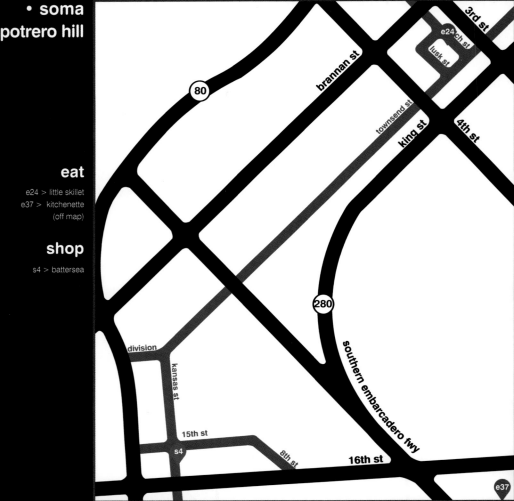

• soma
potrero hill

eat

e24 > little skillet
e37 > kitchenette
(off map)

shop

s4 > battersea

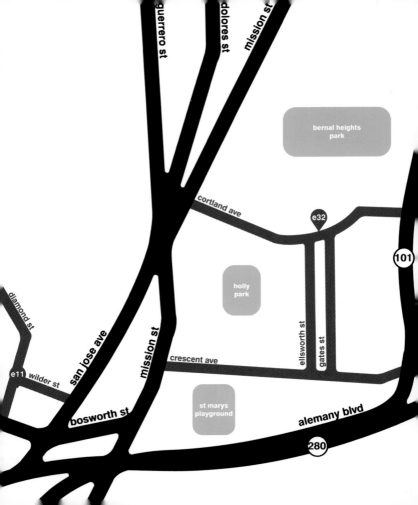

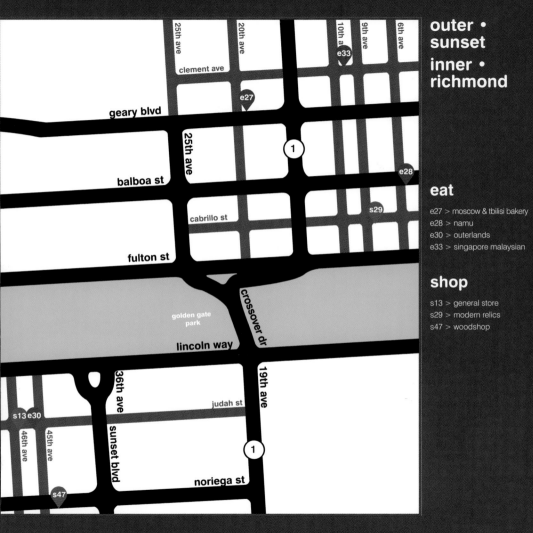

outer •
sunset
inner •
richmond

eat

e27 > moscow & tbilisi bakery
e28 > namu
e30 > outerlands
e33 > singapore malaysian

shop

s13 > general store
s29 > modern relics
s47 > woodshop

note: all maps face north

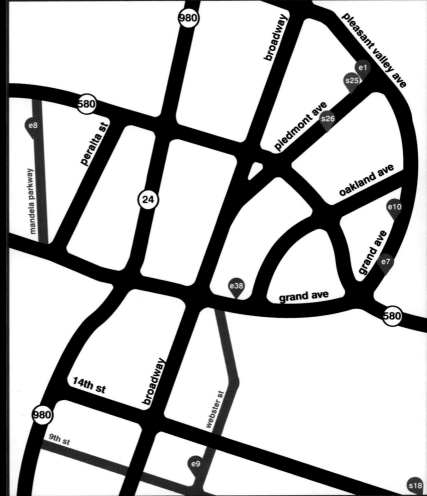

- **oakland**
- **piedmont**
- **lower hills**
- **alameda**

eat

e1 > adesso
e7 > boot and shoe service
e8 > brown sugar kitchen
e9 > cam huong
e10> camino
e38 > true burger

shop

s18 > japan woodworker
(off map)
s25 > mcmullen
s26> mercy vintage now

acrimony

a stylish reality

333 hayes street #102. between franklin and gough
415.861.1025 www.shopacrimony.com
mon, wed - sat 11a - 7p sun noon - 6p

opened in 2008. owner: jenny chung
all major credit cards accepted
online shopping tw: @acrimony

hayes valley > **s01**

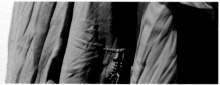

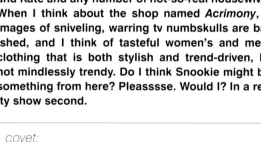

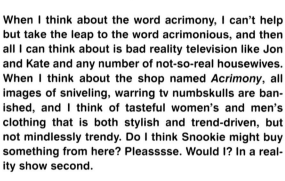

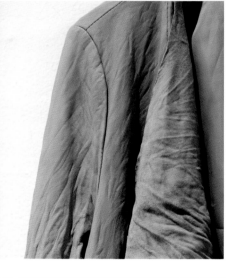

When I think about the word acrimony, I can't help but take the leap to the word acrimonious, and then all I can think about is bad reality television like Jon and Kate and any number of not-so-real housewives. When I think about the shop named *Acrimony*, all images of sniveling, warring tv numbskulls are banished, and I think of tasteful women's and men's clothing that is both stylish and trend-driven, but not mindlessly trendy. Do I think Snookie might buy something from here? Pleasssse. Would I? In a reality show second.

covet:
kaylee tankus
acne
april 77
funktional
rad hourani
wings & horns
gitman brothers
nom de guerre

anica

minimalist women's fashion
2418 polk street. between filbert and union
415.447.4255 www.anicaboutique.com tw: @anicaboutique
tue - fri noon - 7p sat 11a - 6p sun 11a - 5p

opened in 2006. owner: rati sahi
all major credit cards accepted
online shopping

russian hill > **s02**

 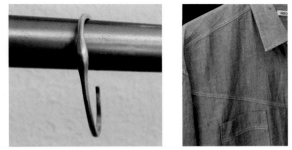

When it comes to my personal style, I have a bit of a split personality. One side will happily sport outrageous Jean Paul Gaultier outfits and towering avant-garde heels. The other side is a minimalist who searches for beautifully-cut clothing with an edge, in muted tones of gray, navy blue and black. Because these days I don't have much call for the Grace Jones side, simplicity and layering is my thing, and *Anica* is where I would outfit that *me*. Don't think that simple = boring; the pieces that *Anica* carries always have a little twist of funk. Perfect for the other *me*.

covet:
anica label
a.p.c.
wood wood
mm6
pensey
rosenmunns
mociun
shin

basil racuk

custom leather bags and accessories

510.409.4452 www.basilracuk.com
by appointment only

opened in 2008. owner: basil racuk
all major credit cards accepted
custom design / orders

no storefront > **s03**

Many years ago my mother and I purchased a beautiful leather shoulder bag together. We have passed it back and forth ever since. But when I buy one of *Basil Racuk's* bags, all of my childhood lessons about sharing are going out the window. Sorry Mom—these custom-made, handcrafted bags demand to be hoarded. Basil, whose design chops have been honed at some iconic American brands, clearly knows his way around a piece of leather. What makes his work so desirable is that it's not machine-made perfect, but full of that handmade quality that signifies a piece of art.

covet:
basil racuk leather goods:
  weekender travel bag
  hard brief
  suspension belt
  computer case
  farmer's market tote
  sling purse
  soft brief

battersea

industrial antiques and beyond

297 kansas street. corner of 16th
415.553.8500 www.batterseasf.com
mon - fri 10a - 5p or by appointment

opened in 2008. owner: will wick
all major credit cards accepted
online shopping (first dibs). design services

potrero hill > 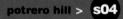 **s04**

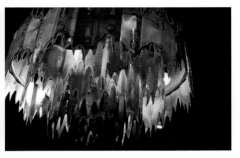

One of these days I'm going to completely start over when it comes to the décor of my house, though starting over is kind of a joke since I never really got started. My husband and I seem to belong to the "sleep-decorating" school of philosophy when it comes our abode. If I could start over, I would choose a style that is modern, but with a good dose of early-to-mid-20th century European and American industrialism thrown in. To find this I would aim for *Battersea*, as Will's collection is the cat's meow. I especially like how he repurposes objects like casters into lamps. Clever man, that Will.

covet:
mounted caster table lamps
brutalist chandelier
leather studded side table
zinc industrial barrels
verdigris floodlight
dental cabinet
fruit wood pear tea caddies
two tier zinc industrial table

belljar

gorgeous little things
3187 16th street. between guerrero and valencia
415.626.1749 www.belljarsf.com tw: @belljarsf
daily noon - 7p

opened in 2008. owner: sasha wingate
all major credit cards accepted
online shopping

mission >  **s05**

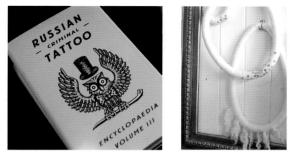

In the last couple of years during the "every day there is a new wave of depressing news," I have (tried) to embrace "the sun will come out tomorrow" approach to life. I think *BellJar's* tagline, "gorgeous little things," ties into my outlook. A lovely object doesn't necessarily need to have a high price tag associated with it—it could be a freshly sprouted tulip or a little jar of glass glitter found at *BellJar*. There are lots of perfect little what-nots here that run the gamut from clothing to jewelry to gifts. I'm feeling sunnier just thinking about it.

covet:
m. graves ceramic tile necklaces
elegantly wasted chain belts
emporium pure glass glitter
kikkerland anatomic pig
thomas paul luddite collection canvas bag
funktional silk wrap play suit
mor beauty products
vintage clothing

bell'occhio

ever enchanting place
10 brady street. between market and stevenson
415.864.4048 www.bellocchio.com
tue - sat 11a - 5p

opened in 1988. owner: claudia schwartz
all major credit cards accepted
online shopping. gift boxes. custom orders / design

<u>upper market</u> > **s06**

I have an alternate universe that exists in my dreams. The Paris of my sleeping hours is vastly different than the real City of Light, so much so that when I visit the city, I'm always looking for the streets in my dreams. Recently I dreamt about *Bell'occhio*, but it was identical to the real one. I'm guessing my subconcious didn't play its usual trick because this place is a dream to behold. Claudia is a brilliant retail storyteller and methodically sources artisan crafted objects that range from ribbons to German chalf to French chapeux. *Bell'occhio* falls firmly into the category of "not too be missed."

covet:
handmade french boxes
l'ecritoire writing set
antique french rock crystal ring
marie antoinette & menagerie
bell'occhio cake stands
loglets
french serviettes
absinthe candles

birch

where flowers and printed matter converge

564 hayes street. between laguna and octavia
3263 sacramento street. corner of presidio
415.626.6860 / 415.922.4724 www.birchsf.com tw: @birchsf
see website for hours

opened in 2007. owners: torryne choate
all major credit cards accepted
custom design / orders. deliveries. installations

hayes valley > **s07**

My first magazine memory was reading *Sunset* in the '70s. By the time I was in high school, I was addicted to *W*. Then came college and I headed to NYC for design school so I could study to become a magazine art director. My obsession peaked during those years and I still have the piles of vintage mags to show for it. So the perfectly curated magazine wall at *Birch* in Hayes Valley is all that and more for me. I should amend that, and say that the "more" refers to the glorious flowers; Torryne is a wizard with the stems. I'll need one arm to carry the mags, and the other to carry a glorious, big bouquet.

covet:
flowers, flowers, flowers
in fiore parfum solide
william eggleston 2 1/4
cocoa absolute
well curated selection of magazines
egg press cards
cowshed frisky cow bath foam
tina frey vases

candystore collective

sweets in the form of clothing and gifts

3153 16th street. between guerrero and valencia
hello: 2226 bush street. between steiner and fillmore
415.863.8143 / 888.601.0117
www.candystorecollective.com tw: @candystorecolle
mon - sat noon - 7p sun noon - 6p

opened in 2005. owner: jennifer jones
all major credit cards accepted
online shopping

mission > s08

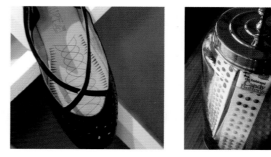

If I didn't make it clear from my drooly love letter to *Miette Confiserie* (page 59), I've got a thing for candy. So if there's a store that's got candy somewhere in its name, there's a good chance that it will be in my good graces, like *Candystore Collective* is. Yes there's candy here, but that isn't what this beloved San Francisco boutique is all about. It is about a kickin' collection of spunky clothing and accessories for both guys and gals. Add a dash of groovy lifestyle items and you've got a recipe for good shopping. And they have a new store called *Hello by Candystore Collective* in the Fillmore District. Sweeeet.

---

covet:
laeken dress
jene d'espain jewelry
yellow owl workshop cards
office wiederholt socks
fluffyco. t's
doily basket
the heated tea towels
cora lyndon jewelry

carrots

gorgeous clothing emporium

843 montgomery street. between jackson and pacific
415.834.9040 www.sfcarrots.com
tue - sat 11a - 6p

opened in 2007. owners: melissa and catie grimm
all major credit cards accepted

jackson square > **s09**

If a carrot is a reward, and a stick the punishment, then the name of this store is quite apropos. Walking in *Carrots* feels like an embarassment of riches. Looking in any direction of this stylish emporium, there's something beautiful to see, and even better to touch, and in the best case scenario, to take home with you. For example, a little something from Tomas Maier would make me feel well rewarded. But am I truly deserving (here comes the stick)? Hold on while I quickly calculate this. I've come to the conclusion that yes, I should get the carrot.

covet:
yigal azrouel
acne
kaufman franco
rick owens
beryll
dusica dusica
jean michel cazabat
cire trudon

cask

artisinal beverage purveyors

17 third street. at market
415.424.4844 www.caskstore.com tw: @caskstore
mon - sat 11a - 7p

opened in 2008. owner: future bars
all major credit cards accepted
online shopping. classes

union square > **s10**

Though I like an icy cold beer while eating spicy food, and I am contractually obligated to drink wine because my husband sells it for a living, what I really like is liquor. Though I could bandy about the "liquor is quicker" cliché, I think that sounds a bit daft coming out of anybody's mouth over the age of 25. So I'll just say that *Cask* is a great bottle shop with a vast selection of hooch, much of it being of the hard-to-find variety and artisianally crafted. Along with the alcoholic goods are tools of the cocktail trade, which can come in handy when slinging your own drinks.

covet:
tequila querida viejo
conemara peated single malt whiskey
ransom old tom gin
toro albala viejisimo solera sherry
scrappy's grapefruit bitters
zubrowka bison grass flavored vodka
maple muddler
bullet cocktail shaker

clary sage organics

organics to wear and to revive

2241 fillmore street. corner of clay
415.309.5746 www.clarysageorganics.com tw: @clarysageorg
mon - sat 10a - 7p sun 11a - 6p

opened in 2008. owner: patti cazzato
all major credit cards accepted
online shopping. wellness center

pacific heights > s11

Here's the thing I find the hardest about being the owner of a small business that requires 192% of my time: things fall apart. Specifically, my body. There's always an ache or a sniffle or something that's messing with the mechanics. But *Clary Sage Organics* makes me feel there's hope on the horizon. First I would sign up with a wellness coach and take full advantage of some—okay, I might need all—of their wellness solutions like the deep defense tea. And yoga would go on the docket, so some pieces from the Clary Sage yoga collection would be key. I feel better already.

119

eden & eden

whimsical design boutique

560 jackson street. corner of columbus
415.983.0490 www.edenandeden.com
mon - fri 10a - 7p sat 10a - 6p sun noon - 6p

opened in 2006. owners: rachel and chas eden
all major credit cards accepted
online shopping

north beach > **s12**

Though I love my brother, I don't think I could run a business with him. This sibling thing doesn't seem to be a problem though for Rachel and her brother Chas. Their labor of brotherly and sisterly love is the always wonderful, always whimsical design boutique *Eden & Eden*. Every time I visit here it's a guarantee that something (or many things) will make me smile. This visit I was tickled by the John and Yoko mice. I'm still cracking up thinking of them. Seriously though, I never leave without making a purchase. It's impossible to do so. I dare you to try.

covet:
cheeky mice
tatty devine pins & necklaces
vintage enamel necklaces
bus roll - 140 harrow
ivana helsinki anything
turquoise wine goblets
donna wilson fox cushion
alice eden gold mesh necklace

general store

just what the name says, but with a modern aesthetic

4035 judah street. between 45th and 46th
415.682.0600 www.visitgeneralstore.com
tue - fri noon - 8p sat 10a - 8p sun 10a - 6p

opened in 2009. owners: mason st. peter and serena mitnik-miller
all major credit cards accepted
custom design / orders

outer sunset > **s13**

There's many a thing I like about this neck of the woods near Ocean Beach. As already noted, I like (love) *Outerlands*, and *Trouble Coffee* is pretty swell. I like the brine in the wind that's whipping off the ocean. And I like (with a couple of exclamation points) *General Store*. SF has a couple of really great, smartly-curated design shops, and this is certainly one of them. With its skatepark meets Santorini interior architecture and products that are just as eclectic, I would happily make the drive out here to take a gander.

covet:
jenny pennywood bags
hakusan porcelain
vintage dairy site glass
manimal moccasins
the printmaking bible by ann d'arcy hughes
two birds fly repurposed skateboards
jesse schlesinger greenhouse
tellason denim

gravel & gold

beautiful bohemia

3266 21st avenue. corner of lexington
415.552.0112 www.gravelandgold.com tw: @gravelandgold
tue - sat noon - 7p sun noon - 5p

opened in 2009. owners: lisa foti-straus, nile nash and cassie mcgettian
all major credit cards accepted
online shopping. classes. customized services

mission > **s14**

Gravel & Gold is the modern equivalent to a coffee klatch sans the coffee. The day I was in here shooting and chatting, the three owners were animatedly esconced in an ever-revolving social hive of interaction. Every person who came through the door was warmly greeted, whether friend or stranger, and soon became part of the conviviality. Each owner in turn became like a docent, talking about the provenence of each item, whether it be a piece of jewelry, a stripey t-shirt or a wall-hanging. I think *Gravel & Gold* is truly the bees knees.

covet:
peterboro ash bike baskets
unison tileworks
deadstock osborn & woods silkscreened cards
tripp carpenter wishbone chair
gravel & gold leather totes & pillows
robert p. miller stripey t's
bergamot brassworks belts
sharon leton beaded auntie earrings

gypsy honeymoon

romantic antiques with a story to tell
1266 valencia street. between 23rd and 24th
415.821.1713
tue - sat 11a - 7p sun 11a - 6p

opened in 1993. owner: gabrielle ekedal
cash only

mission > **s15**

Though I was tempted to use some of the lyrics from Kim Carnes' song "Gypsy Honeymoon" to use here, they are too high on the scmaltz scale to co-opt. So I'll have to use my own words to talk about this beloved Mission antiques and curiosities shop. Though it's changed hands over the years and moved locations, the essence of *Gypsy Honeymoon* has stayed true to its ornate, romantic, a little macabre, Victoriana sensibilities. Gabrielle is a talented retail storyteller creating intriguing vignettes that leave the shopper pondering the tales behind these little snippets of days gone by.

covet:
guatemalan conquistador maps
albumen prints
alligator buttons
1900's glass domes
jes feuny talismans
french grave marker
140-million-year-old amonite
ivory coast hornbill figure

ichiban kan

practical japanese items
22 peace plaza #540 (on post street). between webster and laguna
415.409.0472 www.ichibankanusa.com
daily 10:30a - 8p

opened in 2000. owner: keiji ohshita
all major credit cards accepted

japantown > **s16**

Ichiban Kan is a danger to my bank account. Leave me alone in here for 30 minutes with an unlimited budget to spend, and I would go bonkers. Oh wait, I did go bonkers in here for 30 minutes at my last visit, and I'm not broke. The brilliance of *Ichiban Kan* is you don't need an unlimited budget—think of it as an Asian dollar store. You'll find folks crowding the aisles here for everything from ramen and panko breading to cola-scented erasers and rice ball makers. I'm itching to go as I'm just writing this. I've got the *Ichiban Kan* fever.

covet:
smile mini sauce bottles
country kitchen gingham bento boxes
apple chan lip cream
slimity roller for body
baby foot deodorant spray
happy hot body warmers
p'tit moi oil blotting papers

jak home

a vision for modern living
2423 polk street. between filbert and union
415.348.8088 www.jak-home.com tw: @jakhome
mon - fri 2 - 6p sat - sun 11a - 5p

opened in 2008. owners: jeffrey holt and kathleen navarra
all major credit cards accepted
design services

russian hill > 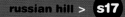 **s17**

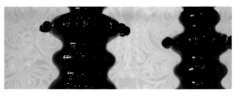

Over the holidays I spent a lot of time in other people's houses throwing *eat.shop at home* parties. Though I've never felt anything but love for my house, after spending time in these gorgeously decorated abodes, I got a big whopping complex. I was shocked into the realization that my house décor was still firmly planted in "just getting a grip that I'm an adult and have randomly decorated my house" style. Oi. I need Jeff and Kathleen's help. If their little Russian Hill showcase (which fronts Navarra Design Studio) was transferred into my house, I guarantee my complex would disappear. Just like that.

covet:
reagan hayes furniture
oly studio stools
robert true vice lamp
juliska glass
arteriors sabine table lamp
dransfield & ross driftwood side table
roost pop can vases
pelican oil painting

japan woodworker

beautifully crafted tools
1731 clement avenue. near grand
510.521.1810 www.thejapanwoodworker.com tw: @japanwoodworker
mon - sat 9a - 5p

opened in 1979. owner: fred damsen
all major credit cards accepted
online shopping. knife sharpening

alameda > **s18**

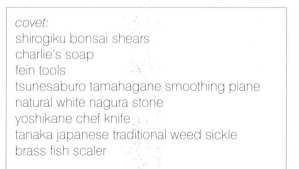

I like handcrafted tools, which is a bit kooky because I'm not really into the activities behind using these tools. For example, at *Japan Woodworker* there is a beautiful forest axe made by the Swedish company Gransfors Bruks. I would love to own this axe, but my pathetic arm strength wouldn't get it over my shoulder. No matter—I still covet it. After spending time wandering the aisles here with Jack, the resident knife sharpener and man of much knowledge, I had pipe dreams of making a kitchen table, carving a totem pole and becoming a sushi chef using tools found here. Just call me a dreamer.

covet:
shirogiku bonsai shears
charlie's soap
fein tools
tsunesaburo tamahagane smoothing plane
natural white nagura stone
yoshikane chef knife
tanaka japanese traditional weed sickle
brass fish scaler

kayo books

vintage paperbacks and pulp fiction
814 post street. between hyde and leavenworth
415.749.0554 www.kayoboks.com
thu - sat 11a - 6p or by appointment

opened in 1995. owners: maria mendoza and ron blum
all major credit cards accepted
online shopping

tenderknob > **s19**

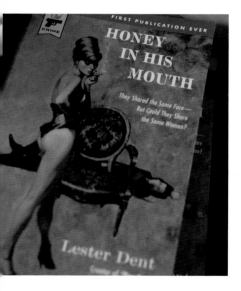

In my mind, pulp fiction falls into two categories: the Quentin Taratino movie of the same name and paperback books from the '40s to '70s with cover illustrations of swooning vixens and gumshoe detectives. I'm leaving a lot to be desired in my description, but I think you get the idea. You'd get an even better idea of the genre if you visited *Kayo Books*. For fans of pulp, this place is the motherlode, along with a vast selection of vintage sci-fi, sleaze and mystery books and/or titles that the legendary H.P. Lovecraft would call "weird fiction." It's all stranger than fiction here.

covet:
honey in his mouth by lester dent
the doc savage series
off-color good humor by juliet lowell
the man who said no by walt grove
dell mapbacks
anything by:
  h.p. lovecraft
  jim thompson

lemon twist

fresher than fresh women's clothing

537 octavia boulevard. between hayes and grove
415.558.9699 www.lemontwist.net
tue - sat 11a - 6:30p sun noon - 5p

opened in 2005. owners: danette and eric scheib
all major credit cards accepted
custom design / orders. shopping salon

hayes valley > **s20**

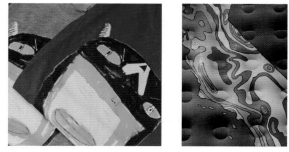

I get a little Kaie shui when a place feels just right to me. For example, *Lemon Twist*. My Kaie shui is off the charts here. Danette's women's clothing line is the essence of West Coast cool girl. It's tailored enough to look sharp, but it's also easy to wear (not to be confused with "easy wear"). And to add to that, you can work with her to customize a piece or two or three. Danette isn't the only talented member of the family though, hubby Eric's artwork is on display and their young son has his hand in t-shirt production. What an awesome family.

covet:
lemon twist:
  516 painted poplin
  615 disco dress
  322 high waisted jean
t's:
  sea of love
  captain america
eric scheib art

little otsu

artist collaborative
849 valencia street. between 19th and 20th
415.255.7900 www.littleotsu.com tw: @littleotsu
daily 11:30a - 7:30p

opened in 2000. owners: yvonne chen and jeremy crown
visa. mc
online shopping

mission >  s21

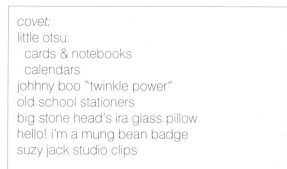

I was well into my fourth year of publishing *eat.shop* before I accepted the fact that I was a publisher. After spending my entire career as an art director and designer, the title of publisher seemed odd and old-fashioned. But this biz has changed in the last decade, and there's lots of super duper creative little publishing houses out their launching fresh work. *Little Otsu* is the perfect example, collaborating with stellar artists and designers to produce whimsical illustrated books and paper goods. Yvonne and Jeremy are so good at what they do, they make this publishing thing look easy. I'm jealous.

covet:
little otsu:
   cards & notebooks
   calendars
johnny boo "twinkle power"
old school stationers
big stone head's ira glass pillow
hello! i'm a mung bean badge
suzy jack studio clips

lola

loveliness for your home and self

2950 college avenue. near ashby
510.981.8345 www.lolahome.com
tue - fri 11a - 6p sat - sun 11a - 5p

opened in 2006. owner: lois vinsel
all major credit cards accepted
custom design / orders. design services

berkeley > **s22**

I have a built-in bias when it comes to *Lola*. This temple of good design shares the same name with my daughter, and though it's not possible for me to like this lovely place as much as my one-and-only daughter, it's definitely captured my shopping affection. Lois has created a retail sanctuary that's hard to leave once you are enveloped in its warmth. Her incredible curatorial eye means each item is better than the next, whether it be the world's most comfortable modern rocking chair or the take-it-with-you fireplace. I heart (both) the *Lolas*.

covet:
house line:
  the lola chaise
  breadboards
livingstones
saipua soaps
michele delucchi flora pendant
herbert hoover ice cream sandwich paperweight
tamar mogendorff stitchworks

lotus bleu

colorful home décor
325 hayes street. at franklin
415.861.2700 www.lotusbleudesign.com
mon - fri 11a - 6p sat 11a - 7p sun noon - 5p

opened in 2006. owner: jeannie fraise
visa. mc
online ordering. custom orders / design. design services

hayes valley > **s23**

Spring has finally arrived and I'm looking outside my window at rows of bright yellow, purple, red and orange tulips. And I'm immediately transported back to *Lotus Bleu*. Walking in here feels like like a tulip field translated into furniture and rugs and bedding and home accessories. If your inclination is to live in a house swathed in stainless steel and tones of greige, the *Lotus Bleu* might make you rethink your decorating style as it's so seductively happy to be surrounded by all this color. And just about everything you see is customizable and made-to-order. Color me pretty.

covet:
custom order:
  settee
  danish rocker
  pillows
muskhane wool felt rugs
madeline weinrib tibetan carpets
john robshaw bedding
kanik chung bird vases

mac

modern appealing clothing for men and women
387 grove street. between franklin and gough
415.863.3011 www.modernappealingclothing.com
mon - sat 11a - 7p

opened in 1980. owners: chris and ben ospital
all major credit cards accepted

hayes valley > 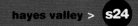 **s24**

Here's a little history of 1980: Mount St. Helens blew, spewing ash to the moon and back, Bjorn Borg beat John McEnroe to win Wimbledon, John Lennon left this world and *Modern Appealing Clothing* came to be. Though most of these people or things are now footnotes of history, *MAC* is still around, fresher and more cutting-edge then ever. I always look forward to visiting here to see Chris and Ben's discoveries, and though they champion established designers like Dries Van Noten, they are always pushing the envelope and introducing new talents. *MAC*, now and forever, makes fashion fun.

covet:
yoshi kondo
dries van noten
sofie d'hoore
dema
walter van beirendonck
engineered garments
sunny sports
kzo

mcmullen

pretty is as pretty does
4395 piedmont avenue. near pleasant valley
1235 grand avenue. near fairview
510.420.6906 / 510.658.6906 www.shopmcmullen.com
mon - sat 11a - 6p

opened in 2007. owner: sherri mcmullen
all major credit cards accepted
personal shopping. alterations

piedmont > 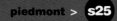 **s25**

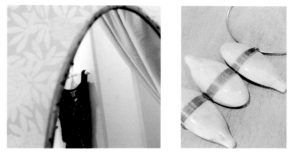

When I was little, even though I was a bit of a tomboy, I liked to dress up. When I moved to New York to go to college, I didn't wear a pair of jeans for four years. Today, though I spend most of my time hunched over a computer, I still love a good reason to wear pretty clothing. And when shopping for said lovelies, *McMullen* would be my first stop. Here I would find a cornucopia of dresses and other pieces that would fit the bill for everything from a dress to wear to work to a outfit for a night out on the town. And for my more casual side, I would visit their new outpost down the hill.

covet:
ports 1961
rag & bone
3.1 philip lim
vince
diane von furstenberg
by malene birger
loeffler randall
kingsley

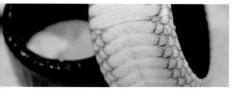

mercy vintage now

well-edited vintage

4188 piedmont. corner of linda
510.654.5599 www.mercyvintage.com tw: @mercyvintagenow
mon - sat 11a - 7p sun noon - 6p

opened in 2009. owners: jenny della santa and karen anderson
all major credit cards accepted
online shopping

piedmont >  **s26**

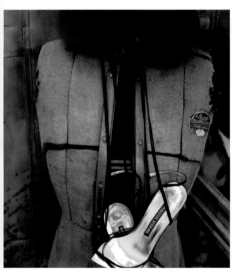

William Shakespeare wrote long ago, "Nothing emboldens sin so much as mercy." If sin be shopping, then yes, *Mercy Vintage Now* emboldens me on to do so. Jenny and Karen have done a fantastic job turning this little corner space on Piedmont Ave. into a vintage clothing destination. They've chosen their collection well, ranging from high-end designer to '70s denim and everything in between. And because it's always a wise idea to mix up vintage with contemporary, there are some modern items like repurposed t-shirts thrown in for good measure. Mercy me.

covet:
vintage:
  norma kamali
  lilli diamond
  courrèges
  gaultier
  qualicraft shoes
anna reutinger modified t's
elisa bongfeldt jewelry

metier

fashion-forward clothing for women

355 sutter street. between stockton and grand
415.989.5395 www.metiersf.com tw: @metiersf
mon - sat 10a - 6p

opened in 1992. owner: sheri evans
all major credit cards accepted

union square > 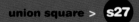 **s27**

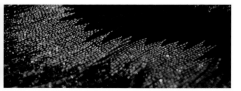

Every woman I know has a couple of go-to spots where they buy their clothing. In this town, a name that pops up on many ladies' go-to lists is *Metier*. Just looking at the designer line-up on the website makes it easy to understand why so many fashionable SFers shop here, as it's a whos-who of the freshest talents in the fashion world. In fact if I was going to open up a women's clothing boutique tomorrow, my wish list of lines would look pretty darn close to *Metier's*. Don't worry though Sheri, I'd rather shop here.

covet:
zero + maria cornejo
isabel marant
steven allan
rachel comey
jeffrey montiero
no. 6
jeanine payer
philip crangi

mi

avant garde bespoke clothing for both sexes

808 sutter street. corner of jones
415.567.8080 www.themiconcept.com
mon - wed by appointment thu - sat 11a - 7p sun 12:30 - 4p

opened in 2008. owner: dean hutchison
all major credit cards accepted
custom design / orders

tenderknob > s28

I think it's hard for some people to embrace the unknown. Instead of mysterious being a word that enthralls, it petrifies. I'm not one of those, and when it comes to clothing, the more smoke and mirrors the better. Which is why *Mi* intrigues me. Dean creates luxe, sharply tailored, slighty avant-garde clothing for both sexes. This is the type of clothing when worn would stop strangers dead in their tracks on the snobby streets of NYC, Paris, London and Tokyo. But there is a price for this type of bespoke brilliance, and I for one, would be willing to pay for it.

covet:
mi:
  scarf jacket
  leather sarong skirt
  high collar fitted jacket
  loose draped vest
  urban halter
  pleated neck coat
  made-to-measure jean

modern relics

time worn objects translated into exquisite jewelry

771 cabrillo street. near eighth
415.422.0477 www.alixbluh.com
mon - wed by appointment or chance thu - sat noon - 7p

opened in 2006. owner: alix blüh
visa. mc
custom design / orders

inner richmond > **s29**

When it comes to guides, I get a laugh when the term off-the-beaten-path is used. At risk of sounding like a guide curmudgeon, almost all the *paths* in big cities are *beaten* pretty quickly, especially in this era of Twitter. So even though *Modern Relics* is tucked away on a quiet street, I'm not going to pretend I discovered it. I will though, take ownership of how fantastic I think it is. Alix has transformed her jewelry workshop into an enchanted den that highlights the heirloomesque quality her work and the complimentary designs that tell the rest of the retail story. I'd beat a path here if I were you.

covet:
alix bluh:
  stag horn earrings
  bramble bracelet
  benevola necklace
  eyeris necklace
diana fayt ceramics
swallow gilt paintings
suga jewelry

nest

an exciting retail journey
2300 fillmore street. corner of clay
415.292.6199 www.nestsf.com
mon - fri 10:30a - 6:30p sat 10:30a - 6p sun 11a - 6p

opened in 1995. owners: judy gilman and marcella madsen
all major credit cards accepted
registries

pacific heights > 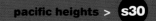 s30

I can't lie. I am nuts about *Nest*, which is why it's featured in this book for a third consecutive edition. I'm sure some would say this reeks of favoritism and they would be absolutely right. But I couldn't tell as compelling an SF shopping story if this legendary boutique was left out. Therefore it's in. Again. And what makes *Nest* so damn special that I'm willing to go out on this limb? When you enter here, you are transported beyond this city. One moment you're in India, next Sweden, then China. It's like having a round-the-world airline ticket all at one address.

covet:
chiratorn dhira pravati vases
oleana blankets & beanies
patch scarves
let me be dress
lisa corti bedding
danielle wellman jewelry
pura ferria jewelry
books, books, books

nomade exquis

stunningly bold vintage jewelry
415.888.8398 www.nomadeexquis.com
by appointment only

opened in 2008. owner: mo clancy
all major credit cards accepted
online shopping. sourcing

no storefront > **s31**

I'm studying the striking business card for *Nomade Exquis*. It's the image of a woman's naked upper torso wearing a bold exclamation point of a necklace. It's the perfect image for the stunning vintage jewelry that Mo sells. Many of these pieces are incredibly powerful and can stand alone as an artistic statement, but when they interact with the curves of a human body, they come alive. Even if your taste runs to more classical or delicate body adornments, you'll find it hard not to be drawn to the strength of this jewelry. When I slipped a bracelet on I felt like Athena—empowered and bold.

covet:
robert larin
ernendes
guy vidal
alfred karram
jorma laine
betty cooke
pentti sarpaneva
de paissille-sylvestre

oak barrel winecraft

beer and winemaking supplies

1443 san pablo avenue. corner of page
510.849.0400 www.oakbarrel.com
mon - fri 10a - 6p sat 10a - 5p

opened in 1957. owner: bernie rooney
all major credit cards accepted
online shopping. classes

berkeley > **s32**

Not long after meeting my husband, I joined him in Barbaresco, Italy to take part in the grape harvest. We spent a couple of weeks having a blast working at friends vineyards, eating great food and, yes, drinking some spectacular wine. Other than the Cabernet grapes, which were a pain in the ass to pick, the whole experience was amazing—so much so that I began to harbor a wee fantasy about making wine. And I could have gotten everything I needed at *Oak Barrel Winecraft* right down to the grapes, and also the fixings for beer, sake and vinegar making. Must get on this.

covet:
hops:
  mt. hood
  styrian golding
british porter kit
vinegar making kit
sake homebrew kit
grape listings
casks

omnivore books on food

new, antiquarian and collectible cooking tomes
3885a cesar chavez street. corner of church
415.282.4712 www.omnivorebooks.com tw: @omnivorebooks
mon - sat 11a - 6p sun noon - 5p

opened in 2008. owner: celia sack
visa. mc
events

noe valley > s33

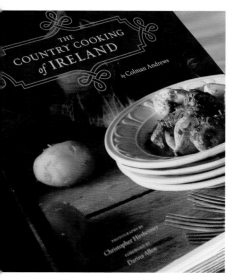

Why are cookbooks so seductive? Let me rephrase that question. Why aren't there more great cookbook stores? Answer to question one: because they are about food, and food is the ultimate seduction. Answer to question two: I have absolutely no idea, but thank goodness Celia opened the wonderful, verging on perfection (I'm trying to think what the flaw is, but can't come up with anything) *Omnivore Books*. If you love food, and love to cook, then this little spot will bedazzle you. Or if you are like me and are attracted to pretty pictures married with well-written prose, then again, thank you Celia.

covet:
encyclopedia of pasta by oretta zanini de vita
cheesemonger: a life on the wedge by
    gordon edgar
kaiseki by yoshihiro murata
cooking on a ration or food is still fun by
    marjorie mills burns
ottolenghi cookbook by yotam ottolenghi
free-range tomales eggs

rare device

lotsa good stuff
1845 market street. between guerrero and pearl
415.863.3969 www.raredevice.net tw: @twotarts
tue - sat noon - 7p sun noon - 6p

opened in 2007. owners: rena tom and lisa congdon
all major credit cards accepted
online shopping

upper market >  **s34**

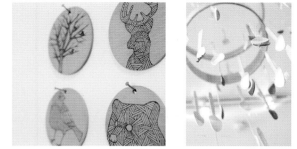

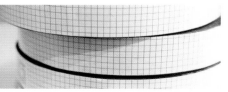

Twitter is a seductive virtual beast. I tried to keep away from it for awhile, but then it sucked me in like a tornado and I started fishing around for people or places that had something interesting to say or to show. At some point Lisa Congdon, an SF illustrator popped up and her tweets fulfilled both my criteria so I followed. Then I realized (duh) that Lisa was one of the owners of *Rare Device* with Rena of the original outpost in NYC. Suddenly Twitter seemed useful, just as *Rare Device* is if you like smart, well-curated design shops as much as I do.

covet:
kimura glass droplet
prismera jewelry
portland general store men's fragrances
roost floating feather ornaments
sagaform mortar & pestle
ideaco & associates coin storage
lisa congdon birch tree notebook
paume's *san francisco kitchens*

story boxes

elaborate, heirloom quality story and shadow boxes

415.221.2682 www.juliehaas.com
by appointment only

opened in the '80s. owner: julie haas
cash only
custom design / orders

no storefront > **s35**

There I was scouring the mean streets of Presidio Heights, when I saw a window display next to a dry cleaners, which held an exquisitely ornate box. There was a calligraphed note that said *Story Boxes* and a phone number. I was hooked. But where was this *Story Boxes* store? Was it in the back of the dry cleaners? Turns out there is no store. Just Julie making both story and shadow boxes to order using your stories and treasured mementos, and her talent and vast supply of artistic materials. Take note—these are heirloom quality pieces and are priced as such. But they are worth every penny.

covet:
custom designed:
  story boxes
  shadow boxes

super7

urban vinyl and more
1628 post street. between webster and laguna
415.409.4700 www.super7store.com tw: @super7store
see website for hours

opened in 2004. owners: brian flynn and dora drimalas
all major credit cards accepted
online shopping

japantown > 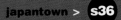 **s36**

As a kid, I used to have nightmares about Godzilla and Mothra and their epic battles. In my dreams, they were in my backyard demolishing the slip n' slide hill and tire swing. Ever since, I've had a hang up with these two. But when I went into *Super7*, I was drawn to a resplendent glow-in-the-dark, urban vinyl Mothra. Suddenly all my *kaiju* (Japanese for strange beast or monster) angst was gone, replaced with a desire to buy buy buy. And not just toys, but the design and and urban culture books, with a t-shirt or two thrown in for good measure.

covet:
super7 toys & t's
hybrid home secret service pillow
us toys booska ramen
gargamel globby
m1go mothra
arbito patty power
fifty24sf t's
on tender hooks by isabel samaras

the bone room

a natural history store

1569 solano avenue. near peralta
510.526.5252 tw: @boneroom
www.boneroom.com / www.boneroompresents.com
tue - sat 11a - 6p

opened in 1987. owner: ron cauble
visa. mc
online shopping. classes. rentals. events / gallery at the bone room presents

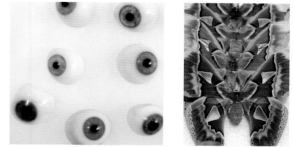

I like things like taxidermy and exotic bugs, like the thorny devil stick, framed in shadow boxes. Though this sounds somewhat macabre and Joel-Peter Witkinesque, I'm too prudish to get all wrapped up in the dark side. I just like natural history, and *The Bone Room* in all its quirky glory, embraces just that. Ron is the one of those über-smart Homo sapiens who should be able to be checked out at the library. He'll happily engage and teach everybody from school kids buying their first fossil to serious collectors looking for ancient hyena skulls. *Gratia*, Ron.

covet:
raccoon tails
goliath beetles
giant marshall islands clam
stiff by marcy roach
dinosaur coprolites
budget skeletons
genuine spider webs
porphorymonas gingivalis (bad breath plushy)

the brooklyn circus

a unique urban style for men

1521 fillmore street. near geary
415.359.1999 www.thebkcircus.com tw: @thebkcircussf
tue - sat noon - 7p sun noon - 6p

opened in 2008. owners: gabriel garcia and ouigi "the bearded man" theodore
all major credit cards accepted
online shopping

western addition > 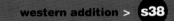 **s38**

As much as I love a guy who can wear a pair of Levi's and a white t-shirt with unaffected panache, I also love a man who can peacock a bit, but not in a Vegas, silk-screened collared, striped shirt untucked sort of way. I'm talking *The Brooklyn Circus* style. While I was shooting here, I was chit-chatting with Gabe and Calvin and was struck by how they wore their *BKC* togs, mixing vibrant colors with patterns in a super fresh, urban updated "Cooleyhighharmony" type of way. There's a tribe of *BKC* types out there, growing steadily nationwide, and panache is their middle name.

covet:
the brooklyn circus:
  varsity jackets
  gatsby cap
  reversible bow ties
  velour cardigans
  denim duffle
sebago boots
happy socks

the curiosity shoppe

crafts, kits and curios for the creatively inclined

855 valencia street. between 19th and 20th
415.671.5384 www.curiosityshoppeonline.com tw: @cshoppe
tue - sat noon - 7p sun noon - 6p

opened in 2007. owners: lauren smith and derek fagerstrom
all major credit cards accepted
online shopping

mission >

Though I may well be running out of interesting things to say as I come towards the end of writing this book, I could never run out of things to say about *The Curiosity Shoppe*. The happiest place on earth comes to mind (sorry Disneyland) whenever I step foot in here. What sets off my feel good bells? It's the goodies that Derek and Lauren choose. As you explore here, you'll see that there's lots of artistically driven, small-run or hand-crafted items, many of them with a cheeky sense of humour lodged into their dna. This is a happy making place.

covet:
jacqueline dufresne apple jacket
sighn "its okay"
katarina häl poem cup & saucer
ukulele kit
a field guide to weeds by kim beck
nous savons 1# necklace
leaf cutter designs wiggly eye dice
slingshot pencil

the gardener

gardening gear and so much more

1836 fourth street. near hearst
1 ferry building. end of market
510.548.4545 / 415.981.8181 www.thegardener.com
see website for hours

opened in 1984. owner: alta tingle
all major credit cards accepted
registries. classes

berkeley > **s40**

I really do (someday) want to garden. The thought of it is incredibly appealing, but every time I gaze at my parking strip with its carefully cultivated urban blend of weeds, I get discouraged. Coming to *The Gardener* does inspire me to buck up, spread some seeds and get dirty. This is an alluring place, not just for the items that inspired the name, but all of the other home and lifestyle pieces here. I now have aspirations beyond the outdoors thanks to *The Gardener*. I also aspire to wear Zaya's leather cuffs while gardening.

covet:
franchi seeds
alessi watering can
mango wood plates
fermob outdoor furniture
zen zen vetiver tassle
teroforma whiskey rocks
japanese rakes
tuscan terra cotta

the perish trust

art, antiques and amusement
728 divisidero street. between fulton and grove
415.400.5225 www.theperishtrust.com
see website for hours

opened in 2008. owners: kelly ishikawa and rod hipskind
cash only

western addition > 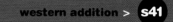 **s41**

One of my favorite things to do as a kid was to go out to my grandparents' farm and spend hours rummaging through their 100-year-old barn. It was shadowy in there, so it was always a bit scary (was I worried about a ghost cow?), but once I got to digging through the years of stored antiques and what nots, all worries disappeared. Poking through *The Perish Trust* brought back memories, though it doesn't smell like hay. Kelly and Rod have collected an eclectic assortment of antiques and ephemera, and intermixed it with local artists' work. Sorry there's no ghost sheep, though.

covet:
mariele williams jewelry
andre nigoghossian glass
jessica niello paintings
kirsten finkas watercolors
kevin randolph lighting
nell van vost ceramics
hooker's sweet treats
antiques & ephemera

timeless treasures

a comely little haven of good things

2176 sutter street. between steiner and pierce
415.775.8366 www.timelesstreasuressf.com
mon - sat 11a - 6p sun 1 - 5p

opened in 1998. owner: joan o'connor
visa. mc

lower pacific heights > **s42**

I love my job, and luckily I do, because complaining about eating and shopping for a living would put me into the big whiners' hall of fame. And when I meet someone who is as enthusiastic about what they do like Joan, I just want to sit down and shoot the breeze. From the moment we started talking, I knew we were like-minded types, as she loves nothing better than exploring a city, sniffing about all of the nooks and crannies. And when you visit her charming retreat of both vintage goods and new, *Timeless Treasures*, you'll be the beneficiary of her hunting skills.

covet:
viva vivande wooden cutting board
vintage letters and lots of 'em!
studiopatró tea towels
vintage musical instrument rubber stamps
vintage blue display hutch
adjowah brodie time flies jewelry
attic journals
la vie parisienne charm bracelets

tradesmen

vintage furnishings to lust for
311 valencia street. near 14th
415.552.8121 ww.tradesmensf.com
by appointment only

opened in 2005. owner: marc joseph
all major credit cards accepted
online shopping (first dibs)

mission > **s43**

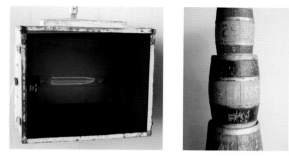

I've always thought of *Tradesmen* like Willy Wonka's chocolate factory. A place where nobody went in, and nobody came out. I have glued my face against the window here for the last six years in hope that somebody, anybody, would appear to open the gates of this little kingdom of vintage goodness. Sadly, nobody came. I suspect there's an indentation in the glass I've pressed my nose against it for so long. And then the great miracle of 2010 happened. The door opened for me. Angels wept. Now that I've entered *Tradesmen*, and touched the beauty, I am complete.

covet:
milo baughman burled olive loveseat
safe light
haberdashery collar display
machine age deco copper "covelite"
painted advertising barrels
mounted sawfish rostrum
john dickinson stone slab lamp
van day truex watercolor

twelve sense media

an exciting, organic collaboration of creative minds
864 post street. between hyde and leavenworth
415.292.5550 www.twelvesensemedia.com
mon - sat 11a - 7p

opened in 2005. owner: matt dick
all major credit cards accepted

tenderknob >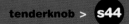

At this point in my production season, my senses have all flat-lined, which is why I need an infusion of Matt and *Twelve Sense Media*. When I spend time with Matt, I come out feeling creatively filled-up because he is the type of person who thinks way, way out of the box. His *Twelve Sense Media* is an example of this, as it's a retail space, studio and think tank, where you'll find a conversation as compelling as a Parisian hand bag. Whatever happens here, its a guarantee it will be ever revolving and ever evolving, leaving boredom in it's wake.

covet:
twelvesensework: workwear
twelvesenselimited:
   accessories, tabletop & printed matter
   2010 lunar calendar
hand loomed indian khadi cloths
meilleur ami bags
len carella ceramics
rare photography & design books

twig & fig

inspired letterpress designs
2110 vine street. between shattuck and walnut
510.848.5599 www.twigandfig.com tw: @twigandfig
mon - sat 10a - 6p

opened in 2004. owners: suzie mckig and serge vigeant
all major credit cards accepted
custom design / orders

berkeley > s45

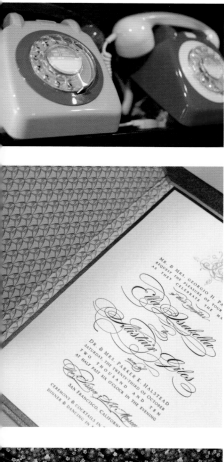

About 15 years ago, I had a hot case of letterpress desire. I had a line on a couple of vintage Heidelbergs, and an idea for a studio. But life intervened, and my letterpress dreams went by the wayside. To this day, I can't be around this craft without getting weak-kneed, which is what happened at *Twig & Fig*. Suzie and Serge are a formidable creative team and make the most outrageously detailed custom invites and accompanying collateral I've ever seen. I had some serious designer envy. But I got over it so I could browse the paperie which has a swell selection of paper goods and lifestyle goodies.

covet:
twig & fig:
  couture invitations
  stationery
  calling cards
penkridge porcelain fruit
screech owl design cards
caran d'ache pens
vintage british telecom phones

unionmade

american and european heritage brands

493 sanchez street. corner of 18th
415.861.3373 www.unionmadegoods.com
mon - fri noon - 7p sat 11a - 7p sun noon - 6p

opened in 2009. owner: todd barket
all major credit cards accepted
online shopping

noe valley >  s46

I am a child of the '70s, and though I experimented with wearing Calvin Kleins and the aforementioned San Francisco Riding Gear, I believe with absolute certainty that Levi's are godhead when it comes to jeans. I take this belief so seriously it brought down a couple of boy-friends who didn't own a pair. And because I believe in these American heritage brands, I can advocate whole-heartedly for *Unionmade*. Todd, who might be one of the ten friendliest people on earth, has created a retail environment for men that carries a stellar collection of these goods. Just makes me wish I was a boy.

covet:
levi's xx brand
american optical
alden
chester wallace
fox river red heel socks
juniper ridge
sns herning
filson

woodshop

an artists collective

3725 noriega street. near 44th
danny: 415.867.3214 / luke: 415.240.5504
www.hesssurfboards.com / www.chairtastic.com
www.jeffcanham.com / www.refindfurniture.com
by appointment only

opened in 2010. owners: danny hess, josh duthie, luke bartels and jeff canham
visa. mc
custom design / orders

outer sunset >  **s47**

Working on these books can be like doing a connect-the-dot puzzle. The first dot in SF was Danny Hess, whose custom-built, wood surfboards caught my eye. I was playing phone tag with him on the day I was shooting *Outerlands* and *General Store*. While in *GS*, I was lusting for a vintage chair and Mason told me that Josh, the designer, had a studio a couple of blocks away with a guy building surfboards. Ding ding ding. I followed the dots to *Woodshop*, a big workspace that also houses Jeff, an amazing sign painter and Luke who handcrafts furniture from reclaimed wood. Dots connected.

covet:
danny hess surfboards
luke bartels re/find furniture
jeff canham hand-painted sign & graphics
josh duthie's chairtastic

etc.

the eat.shop guides were created by kaie wellman and are published by cabazon books

eat.shop san francisco 2nd edition was written, researched and photographed by kaie wellman

editing: kaie wellman   copy editing: eve connell
map and layout production: julia dickey and bryan wolf

kaie thx: sue and sophia for sharing their comfy abode. thx to christian for his chicken and waffles and food cart tips.

cabazon books: eat.shop san francisco 2nd edition
ISBN-13 9780982325483

every effort has been made to ensure the accuracy of the information in this book. however, certain details are subject to change. please remember when using the guides that hours alter seasonally and sometimes sadly, businesses close. the publisher cannot accept responsibility for any consequences arising from the use of this book.

the eat.shop guides are distributed by independent publishers group: www.ipgbook.com

to peer further into the world of eat.shop and to buy books, please visit: www.eatshopguides.com